CHRIST IN THE CLASSROOM

THE CHRISTIAN TEACHER AND THE PUBLIC SCHOOL

ARNOLD BURRON
AND
JOHN EIDSMOE

ACCENT BOOKS
Denver, Colorado

Note: John Eidsmoe is the author of the Introduction and chapters 1-4. Arnold Burron authored chapters 5-8. Chapter 9 is primarily the work of Arnold Burron in collaboration with John Eidsmoe.

ACCENT BOOKS

A division of Accent Publications, Inc.
12100 West Sixth Avenue
P.O. Box 15337
Denver, Colorado 80215

Library of Congress Catalog Card Number 87-70238

ISBN 0-89636-233-7

Second Printing 1989

Contents

If you want to shape the mind of a culture, you begin by shaping its educational system.

Charles Colson
"The Secularization of America"
DISCIPLESHIP JOURNAL
Issue 38, 1987

Introduction

The student stood up in the school assembly. He directed his question to the speaker. "Sir, you've told us all about the problems of our society—drugs, crime, lack of morals, lack of discipline. But what's the solution?"

The speaker paused. He'd been reprimanded before for sharing his faith in the public schools. His reputation had preceded him. Prior to being allowed to speak in this high school, he had had to promise not to mention Jesus Christ. But the question had been squarely put, and there was only one correct answer. All eyes were upon him. He returned the students' gaze, drew a breath, and began his answer.

"I would like to tell you the solution—because a solution does exist. But I can't. You see, the solution is a Person, but because of a policy of the school, I had to promise not to mention His name. So I'll simply refer to this Person as 'You Know Who.' You can read about 'You Know Who' in a certain well-known book that I shouldn't mention either. This book tells us that You Know Who's Father loved the human race so much that He sent You Know Who to live among us, show us the way to live, and die on a cross to pay for our sins. This book also tells us that, after dying on the cross, You Know Who rose from the dead and is with His Father today. He is coming again some day to solve the world's problems and rule the world in righteousness. This Book also tells us the way to personal peace and forgiveness. Believe on You Know Who and thou shalt be saved. That's the solution."

The above incident actually happened. And the students were on the edge of their chairs, their interest piqued by the knowledge that they were getting "forbidden" information. But the speaker has mixed feelings about the ethics of this type of witness and doesn't recommend it to others.

The incident, however, illustrates the dilemma of the Christian teacher in the public school. The Christian teacher, who takes seriously the command of Jesus Christ to "preach the gospel to every creature" (Mark 16:15), realizes that that must include the students in his classrooms. But he must also take seriously his duty to obey his supervisors (Ephesians 6:5), who frequently want controversial matters like "religion" left out of the classroom—sometimes under the mistaken notion that "separation of church and state" requires that God and religion never be mentioned in public.

How does the Christian teacher resolve this dilemma? How can the Christian teacher obey God and also please his human superiors? Can one serve God and Caesar at the same time? Many have tried to solve this problem in various ways.

Some, deciding they must obey God rather than men, have taken a firm stand for the gospel. One teacher, who had been president of the South Dakota Education Association and South Dakota Educator of the Year, decided he must teach the creation account of origins and defied orders from his supervisors to refrain from doing so. Consequently, he was fired. Likewise, a teacher in Florida was fired for reading the Bible to his students in defiance of orders to stop doing so. As a result, these dedicated teachers no longer have the opportunity to share themselves and their faith with their students. Much as we might applaud their courage, we must realistically acknowledge that this is a less than ideal solution.

Others decide to "toe the mark" and refrain from witnessing in the classroom. Some accept as true the erroneous concept that the Constitution requires absolute separation of church and state. They determine that the best way to achieve neutrality is to be totally silent about God and religion. "After all," they reason, "I can still serve the Lord in my church, and in my family, and perhaps in the classroom some of my good Christian example will rub off on others. In the meantime, I have to worry about keeping my job." The problem with such silent Christianity is that while students may see a good example, they have no reason to associate that good example with Jesus Christ. These teachers may be fine Christian people, but as far as the classroom is concerned, they are like a light that is hidden under a bushel, or like salt that has lost its savor (Matthew 5:13-15).

Still others throw up their hands in disgust, decide the public schools are no place for a Christian, and go into private schooling instead. Many dedicated, selfless teachers devote countless hours (often at much reduced salaries) to serving God in Christian schools. We are thankful for them and the Christian parents who give sacrificially to send their children to Christian schools, having paid taxes to support a public system they do not use. Certainly God has called many Christians into private education, and we must commend them for following God's call.

But is *every* Christian called into private education? Must Christians abandon the public schools? Must we surrender the public schools—and the millions of children who attend them—to the forces of secular humanism and worse? Should the public schools be regarded as a Babylonian wasteland in which a Christian has no place?

Guy Doud doesn't think so. In 1986 Guy Doud was named National Teacher of the Year by the National Education Association. Doud teaches in the Brainerd, Minnesota public schools. And he is a committed Christian.

Doud openly credits Jesus Christ with his professional success. "If there is any credit to be given for the success that I've enjoyed as a teacher, it has to go to Jesus Christ. If it weren't for Him, I would not have the same philosophy and attitudes that I have."

An elder in his church, Doud doesn't buy the idea that Christianity must be kept out of the classroom. "My Christian commitment directly affects the way I teach," he says. "My goal is to be as good a Christian at home and in school as I am in church on Sunday morning." [1]

If Guy Doud can make it as a Christian in the public schools,

9

so can you! But to do so requires knowledge.

First, you need to know the law. You need to understand your Constitutional rights as well as the rights of your fellow teachers, your students, and their parents. You need to understand in what ways state and local laws give you rights and in what ways they limit your rights—and you will find that you have more freedom to express yourself in the classroom than many have tried to lead you to believe!

Second, you need practical knowledge of how to witness effectively: What techniques work and what do not; what works at different age levels; handling problems with administrators and parents; et cetera.

This book will give you that knowledge. Author Eidsmoe is a constitutional attorney who has taught Education Law and who has represented parents, students, teachers, administrators and school boards in legal matters throughout the nation. Author Burron is a professional educator who has devoted thousands of hours in the classroom preparing teachers and students alike.

The public schools are perhaps the greatest mission field in the United States today. Within their walls are millions of impressionable children—many of them from Christian homes—who need the input of the Word of God. The teachers who would serve Christ in the public schools must be "wise as serpents, and harmless as doves" (Matthew 10:16). The Christian teacher does face limits in public education, but the limits are not insurmountable. God has not been expelled from the public schools, as some have claimed. He is still there, and He is ready to help His servants in public education.

Our hope and prayer is that this book will be used of God to equip you to serve Him better in public education.

FOOTNOTES

[1] "Teacher of the Year Credits Faith in Christ," Evangelical Press, *Faith and Fellowship*, June 1986, p. 2.

Chapter 1

The Constitution and the Law: A Two-Edged Sword

The debate at the political caucus was becoming heated. A delegate had introduced a resolution calling for respect for teachers' academic freedom and for certain procedural rights to be granted to teachers in the event they were disciplined or fired.

"Teachers are American citizens just like anyone else," declared the man who had introduced the resolution. "They have the same constitutional right to free speech that the rest of us have, and they don't shed that right when they enter the classroom door. Let's stop treating our teachers as though they were second class citizens!"

"I disagree!" countered an opponent. "Where in the Constitution does it say that anyone has a right to teach in the public schools? Teaching in the public schools is a *privilege*, not a *right*. The people of the school district, acting through their elected representatives, the school board, may grant or deny that privilege on whatever conditions they choose. If the people of this school district don't want certain ideas taught, they have every right to make sure their teachers comply. If a teacher isn't willing to teach the way the taxpayers and parents who employ him want him to teach, he shouldn't take the job. He should teach somewhere else, or go into another line of work."

In this exchange we see two contrasting views of the role of a public school teacher. One sees the teacher as a free citizen—like everyone else. The other sees the teacher primarily as an agent of the state. Who is right?

The fact is that there is considerable truth in both positions. And that explains why today's public school teacher is in a dilemma. On the one hand, the teacher *is* an agent of the state. He is hired by the school board, which is an entity created by the state. He is paid by the state, and he utilizes a school building, classroom, texts, and other materials supplied by the state. He teaches before a captive audience of students who dutifully listen to what he has to say, in part because the state's compulsory attendance laws require them to be present. In a very real sense, then, his students are likely to regard what he tells them as the official position of the state.

But at the same time, teachers are people. They are not mere teaching machines. In *Epperson v. Arkansas,* [1] a 1968 case which involved a state law prohibiting the teaching of evolution, the U.S. Supreme Court declared, "It is much too late to argue that the State may impose upon the teachers in its schools any conditions that it chooses, however restrictive they may be of constitutional guarantees." And, a year later in *Tinker v. Des Moines Independent Community School District,* [2] a case involving a school policy prohibiting students from wearing armbands to protest the Vietnam war, the Court said that neither "students nor teachers shed their constitutional rights to the freedom of speech or expression at the schoolhouse gate."

So the teacher is both an agent of the state and a private citizen with constitutional rights. Balancing these dual roles is the difficult task of school boards, school officials, and teachers themselves. When these roles are not balanced correctly, it becomes the duty of the courts to correct that imbalance.

Essentially, the teacher's dual role was perhaps best summarized by the Second Circuit U.S. Court of Appeals in *James v. Board of Education* (1972). [3] That court declared that a teacher is entitled to express his views about things he believes, but he may not indoctrinate his students in a narrow-minded or intolerant manner.

Let us see how this balance is distinguished and preserved in the various provisions of the Bill of Rights, the first ten amendments to the Constitution.

Freedom of Religion

The First Amendment begins, "Congress shall make no law respecting an establishment of religion, or prohibiting the free exercise thereof.... " We divide this guarantee into two parts, the *establishment clause* and the *free exercise clause*.

The authors of the First Amendment probably intended the establishment clause to prevent one denomination from gaining official dominance over others. It was not designed to prevent the government from encouraging religion in general or even Christianity in general. [4] But the courts have given the establishment clause a much stronger interpretation. The courts have used the establishment clause to strike down, among other things, the use of state-composed prayers in public schools, Bible-reading ceremonies, the posting of the Ten Commandments on school walls, and some forms of state aid to private schools. However, other forms of state aid to private schools, the use of nativity scenes on public property at Christmas time, and religious carols in public school Christmas programs have been held not to violate the establishment clause. What's the difference?

In the 1971 *Lemon v. Kurtzman* [5] case, the Supreme Court set forth a three-part test to determine whether government interaction with religion violates the establishment clause: (1) Does the government activity have a secular purpose? (2) Does the government activity have the primary effect of advancing or inhibiting religion? (3) Does the government activity constitute excessive entanglement of government with religion? If the government activity fails any one of these three parts of the test, it will be struck down as unconstitutional.

For example, the singing of carols in a public school Christmas program does not violate the establishment clause provided it is done in good taste and without a clear religious purpose. It passes all three tests. First, the singing of carols has the secular purpose of enhancing the enjoyment of Christmas and familiarizing students with an important part of their cultural heritage. Second, while the singing of carols may have a slight tendency to advance religion, that does not seem to be its *primary* effect. And third, there is little government entanglement with religion, simply the teaching and leading of carols.

Various other activities have failed one or more parts of this test. Each case must be judged on its own merits since the courts have not yet given very clear directions as to how the test will be applied. It is interesting to note that the Supreme Court upheld the display of a nativity scene on public property in 1984, but in 1986 the Court struck down the use of a cross in the official seal of Bernalillo County, New Mexico. In the latter case, the Court reasoned that the cross is primarily a symbol of the Christian religion, but in the earlier case the Court held that manger scenes had become so much a part of the cultural heritage of our people that for most of us they do not have significant religious meaning. It almost appears that the Court is saying religious observances will be permitted so long as they do not have much religious meaning.

It is important to add that the courts are still wrestling with the *Lemon* test (which some lawyers think is appropriately named!), and it is difficult to say whether the courts will interpret this test more narrowly or more broadly, modify it or abandon it altogether. Much will depend upon who is appointed to the courts in years to come.

The free exercise clause protects the citizen's right to believe as he chooses about religious matters and to act upon those beliefs. The freedom to believe is absolute, the Court has said; but the freedom to act upon those beliefs, while protected by the Constitution, is not absolute. [6] It is subject to various restrictions in the public interest.

In *Wisconsin v. Yoder,* [7] a 1972 case involving the Amish and their right to keep their children out of public schools, the Supreme Court articulated a three-part test for applying the free exercise clause: (1) Does the case involve a sincere and deeply held religious belief? (2) Does the government regulation substantially burden the exercise of this religious belief? (3) Does the state have a compelling interest that justifies overriding this religious belief and that cannot be achieved by any less restrictive means?

In *Yoder* there was no question that the Amish were sincere in their beliefs. The Court determined that the compulsory attendance law could have the effect of disrupting the Amish way of life which was based upon religion. It therefore constituted a substantial burden. While the Court recognized that the state has a very strong interest in education (it did not label that interest "compelling"), the court concluded that that interest could be fulfilled while allowing the Amish to keep their children out of the public schools and to teach them at home in their unapproved Amish schools.

One might say that the establishment clause limits the teacher in his official capacity while the free exercise clause protects the teacher as an individual citizen.

At times there can be a certain tension, although not a contradiction, between the two clauses. Consider, for example, the teacher who wants to tell his students how to find salvation through the Lord Jesus Christ. The teacher might argue, and some would agree, that Christ has commanded him to "preach the gospel to every creature" (Mark 16:15). It is, therefore, a matter of religious conviction, and the free exercise clause protects his right to witness in this way. But others might argue that the teacher is a state employee and, therefore, his act of witnessing takes on the appearance of official state endorsement of Christianity. It is the task of the courts to resolve conflicts like these.

Free Speech

The First Amendment doesn't stop with the establishment clause and the free exercise clause. Next comes the *free speech clause.* "Congress shall make no law . . . abridging the freedom of speech . . . . "

In a 1981 case, *Vincent v. Widmar*, [8] the Supreme Court upheld the right of Christian students at the University of Missouri-Kansas City to meet on campus as a religious group. While the case had been argued on many grounds, including establishment and free exercise of religion, the Court ruled in favor of the students on the basis of the free speech clause. The greatest significance of this case is that it establishes that *religious speech is protected under the free speech clause just like any other kind of speech!*

To explain the working of the free speech clause in public schools, it is helpful to understand the concepts of "public forum" and "equal access." "Public forum" or "First Amendment forum" means that certain kinds of public property are considered to be areas in which people may speak freely and exchange ideas about matters of public opinion. Public streets, sidewalks, parks, etc., are usually considered to be First Amendment forums, whereas prisons, military installations, etc., are not. Whether an area is or is not a First Amendment forum depends in large part upon how it has been used in the past. If it is considered a First Amendment forum, public officials must grant "equal access" to all parties; they may not let some groups use the facility and deny the use to others simply because the views of the latter groups are somehow objectionable.

Is a public school a First Amendment forum? The *Tinker* case mentioned earlier indicates that it is, as do several other cases. In *Vail v. Board of Education* [9] a federal district court held that if a public high school provides a forum,

> It must do so in a manner consistent with constitutional principles. Access to the podium must be permitted without discrimination. It is not for the school to control the influence of a public forum by censoring the ideas, the proponents, or the audience. The right of the student to hear a speaker cannot be left to the discretion of school authorities on a pick and choose basis.

If public school officials open their facilities to the expression of ideas generally, they may not refuse one person or group the freedom to meet and express ideas just because those ideas are unpopular with school officials. For the Christian, the significance of these decisions, coupled with *Vincent v. Widmar*, also mentioned above, is that school officials probably may not prohibit Christian teachers, students, or groups from meeting and expressing ideas just because those ideas are religious in nature. If other ideas may be expressed, so may religious ideas. If other groups may meet, so may Christian groups.

The Christian teacher might be well-advised to assert his rights based upon the free speech clause as well as the freedom of religion clauses. There are several advantages in doing so. First, some judges seem to relegate the religion clauses, especially the free exercise clause, to second-class status, although that clearly was not the framers' intent. [10] Those same judges may be more impressed by a free speech claim.

Second, to assert a free exercise claim you must prove that your belief is religious and that it is sincerely and deeply held. There is no such requirement under the free speech clause. This could be especially important on such matters as creation vs. evolution, anti-communism, abortion, or premarital sex. While you may form your views on those subjects from a clearly religious perspective, a court (or school board) might regard them as philosophical or ideological and thus not protected by the free exercise clause.

Third, the obligation to show a substantial burden upon free exercise of religion may not be necessary under a free speech claim. You need only show that the government regulation may have a "chilling effect," that is, a tendency to discourage people from expressing themselves.

Usually it is not necessary to choose one or the other. Generally, you can assert both free exercise and free speech claims at the same time.

Freedom of the Press

The First Amendment continues: " . . . or of the press . . . . " Roughly speaking, this extends the guarantees of the speech clause to printed communications or those which receive widespread distribution through the media.

Normally this will have little effect upon teachers in their official capacities. However, it could protect a teacher in his work with a student newspaper, or the newsletter of a teachers' association, or a communication to the general public about conditions within a school.

Freedom of Assembly

The First Amendment concludes: " ... or the right of the people peaceably to assemble, and to petition the Government for a redress of grievances." This protects your right to meet with others for the purpose of changing government policies. And since the school district is a governmental entity, this includes the right to meet with others to protest school policies.

Under some circumstances the state's interest might override this right, for instance, if it would undercut school discipline. But in most circumstances the school district would have a heavy burden of proof to overcome before it could justify overriding the freedom of assembly.

The Due Process Clause

The Fourteenth Amendment provides, in part, that " ... nor shall any State deprive any person of life, liberty, or property, without due process of law .... " While this pertains specifically to the states, a similar provision of the Fifth Amendment applies to the federal government.

Every teacher has a property interest in teaching, and possibly a liberty interest as well. Even for a non-tenured teacher, the teaching contract is a property interest since it obligates the school district to pay a salary. A tenured teacher has an implied contract that he will be continued as a teacher from year to year unless good cause exists to terminate him. That implied contract is also a property interest.

The school district is an entity of the state. Therefore, the school district cannot deprive you of this property interest (i.e., refuse to renew your contract if you are tenured, or fire you in mid-contract if you are not) "without due process of law."

So what is due process of law? Used in this context, it is the procedural safeguards necessary to ensure that justice is done according to standards of fundamental fairness. It would not, in this context, require a full court trial, but it would certainly involve the right to be told the reasons for termination, the opportunity for a hearing to refute the allegations, the right to consult with legal counsel, and so on.

The due process clause, then, is a guarantee that a teacher will not be arbitrarily fired or otherwise penalized because of his religious beliefs and practices.

The Equal Protection Clause

The Fourteenth Amendment also provides that no State shall "deny to any person within its jurisdiction the equal protection of the laws."

Just as this clause has been used to combat racial discrimination, so it may be used to combat other forms of discrimination as well—including discrimination against Christians. Essentially, the clause means that the State may not discriminate against anyone without a good reason for doing so.

While the Christian teacher cannot expect special privileges because of his faith, he can expect equal and fair treatment. If other teachers are permitted to express pro-abortion opinions in class, the Christian teacher should be permitted to express the opposite point of view. Refusal to allow him to do so is discrimination and a violation of the equal protection clause. If one teacher is permitted to sponsor a study of Shakespeare, the Christian teacher should be permitted to sponsor a Bible study. In short, the Christian teacher has the same right to share his ideas that others have to share theirs.

Other Protections

A teacher's rights are not protected just by the Constitution.

Sometimes federal statutes and regulations may also offer protection, especially for teachers in a federally-funded program. State constitutions often contain constitutional protections that add to or go beyond the U.S. Constitution. State laws, state board of education regulations or guidelines, or local board of education rules may also provide protection for your rights or limitations on your rights. Some state or local boards have adopted regulations that set forth in detail what religious activities may and may not be allowed in the public schools under their jurisdiction. Such regulations are probably valid unless they conflict with state, federal, or Constitutional provisions.

This book will help you understand your rights under the U.S. Constitution. You should also understand what additional rights you may have in your locality. Find out whether your school district has regulations concerning religious practices on campus or freedom of expression, and make sure you understand those rules. Then you will be in a position to exercise them responsibly in the service of your employers, your students, and your Lord.

FOOTNOTES

[1] *Epperson v. Arkansas,* 393 U.S. 97 (1968).

[2] *Tinker v. Des Moines Independent School District,* 393 U.S. 503 (1969).

[3] *James v. Board of Education,* 461 F.2d 566 (2 Circuit 1972).

[4] See generally, Eidsmoe, *The Christian Legal Advisor* (Milford, Michigan: Mott Media, 1984; Grand Rapids: Baker Book House, 1987), pp. 133-164; Joseph Story, *Commentaries on the Constitution of the United States* (Boston, 1833), Vol. 2, sec. 1874, p. 593; James Madison, Floyd's Summary of Congressional Proceedings, August 15, 1789, I *Annals,* p. 730.

[5] *Lemon v. Kurtzman,* 403 U.S. 602 (1971).

[6] *Cantwell v. Connecticut,* 310 U.S. 296 (1940).

[7] *Wisconsin v. Yoder,* 406 U.S. 205 (1972).

[8] *Vincent v. Widmar,* 454 U.S. 263 (1981).

[9] *Vail v. Board of Education,* 354 F. Supp. 592 (D.C.N.H.), VACATED F.2d 1159 (2 Circuit 1972).

[10] Eidsmoe, *The Christian Legal Advisor,* pp. 152-164; Lawrence Tribe, *American Constitutional Law* (Mineola, New York: Foundation Press, 1978), section 14-7, p. 833; section 14-3, p. 818; Chief Justice Warren Burger, Dissenting Opinion, *Meek v. Pittenger,* 421 U.S. 349 (1975).

Chapter 2

A Christian View of Public Education

We live in the midst of what is commonly called the "Me Generation." A glamorous model advertises expensive personal care items on television and assures us, "I'm worth it." Modern psychology urges self-assertion, and the common slogan is, "I've got my rights!" Self-indulgence is the order of the day, and modern American men and women think they can do whatever they want. After all, they say, "It's my body!" and, "It's my life!"

Contrast those sentiments with the words of the Apostle Paul: "... ye are not your own.... For ye are bought with a price: therefore glorify God in your body, and in your spirit, which are God's" (I Corinthians 6:19-20).

Jesus Christ suffered and died on the cross for our sins. In so doing, He paid the penalty for sin and redeemed us from bondage and condemnation. And when we accept that sacrifice, we belong to Him. It is no longer *my* life, or *my* body, or *my* spirit; they belong to the Lord, and they are to be lived and used in His service.

What does this do to the notion, "I've got my rights"? Christians certainly do have rights in civil society—the same rights as other citizens. And, under some circumstances, it is proper for Christians to assert those rights. On several occasions the Apostle Paul did just that (Acts 16:35-40; 21:27-40; 22:22-30; 25:10-12). But he did so, not for himself, but in the service of his Lord. Likewise, the Christian teacher asserts his rights so that he may have more opportunity to witness and serve Christ.

This book does not recommend going to court except when absolutely necessary. Romans 12:18 says, "If it be possible, as much as lieth in you, live peaceably with all men." This includes living peaceably with school boards, principals, and others. Our words and actions are to be living testimonies of Christ in us. However, it is *not* always possible, or right, to ignore the active defense of the gospel. There are times in which a lawsuit is the only alternative, especially if Christian principles and the rights of other Christians are involved. The Apostle Paul was a strong advocate for the gospel, and whenever he was brought before the authorities for his faith, he gave a clear, unashamed witness.

While the Christian teacher does belong to the Lord, he also has obligations to others. He is obligated to serve and obey the school board that hired him, and the superintendent and principal that the school board has placed over him (I Peter 2:18; Ephesians 6:5-8; Colossians 3:22-24). He has a duty to the children in his classroom to make sure they receive the best education possible—academically, morally, spiritually, socially, and in every other way. And, he has a duty to the parents who have placed their children in his care to make sure those children receive the kind of training their parents desire and expect.

This complex arrangement includes at least four parties and four sets of interrelationships, replete with obligations and potential conflicts: teachers, administrators, parents, and children. The rights, needs, and desires of teachers may conflict with those of administrators. Children may want things in school that their parents know is not good for them. The teacher's view of what is best for the children in his care may be different from the parents' views. All sorts of alliances and conflicts can develop: parents and their children against the teacher and administrator; teacher and child against parent; teacher and parent against child; parent and teacher against administrator, and so on. We might conceptualize it like this:

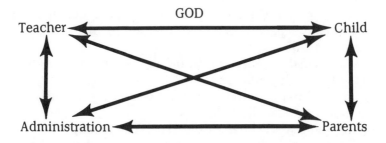

The nature of these conflicting duties and obligations becomes more apparent when we consider the Christian view of education. Traditionally, Christians believe that God is the Author of all knowledge. He is the Creator of the human mind, and it is His will that people develop their minds to their fullest potential.

Christians believe, too, that education should be centered around a Christian world-view—a view that recognizes the Triune God as the Creator and Sustainer of the universe and of all life. It is a view that points to the incarnation, life, death and resurrection of Jesus Christ as the central fact of all history. It identifies God as the Author and Cause of all scientific laws and principles. It is a view that sees the purpose of literature and drama as being the glorification of God; that teaches God and His revelation of Scripture as the source of absolute truth and absolute values, and one that sees the glorification and enjoyment of God as the ultimate purpose of man's existence. As the Psalmist says, "The fear of the Lord is the beginning of wisdom" (Psalm 111:10).

That being the case, academic instruction and spiritual instruction should not be separated. The modern distinction between the sacred and the secular has no basis in Scripture or in Judeo-Christian tradition. The Apostle Paul clearly says that every thought is to be brought into captivity to Christ (II Corinthians 10:5). To try to separate the academic from the spiritual leads to an intellectual schizophrenia in which Christ is Lord of some thoughts but not others. The repeated references to "truth" in Scripture (John 17:17; Philippians 4:8; etc.) in no way separate "sacred" truth from "secular" truth; both are seen as God's truth.

The 1914 *Catholic Encyclopedia* offered the following as basic tenets of Catholic education:

1. Intellectual education must not be separated from moral and religious education....

2. Religion should be an essential part of education; it should form not merely an adjunct to instruction in other subjects, but the centre about which these are grouped and the spirit by which they are permeated. The study of nature without any reference to God, or of human ideals with no mention of Jesus Christ, or of human legislation without Divine law is at best a one-sided education....

3. Sound moral instruction is impossible apart from religious instruction....

4. An education which unites the intellectual, moral and religious elements is the best safeguard for the home, since it places on a secure basis the various relations which the family implies....

5. Far from lessening the need of moral and religious training, the advance in educational methods rather emphasizes that need....[1]

This has also been the historic Christian position for centuries. Martin Luther, whose views on education were generally typical of early Protestants, recognized the need for God-centered education:

Above all things, the principal and most general subject of study, both in the higher and lower schools, should be the Holy Scriptures.... But where the Holy Scripture does not rule I certainly advise no one to send his child. Everyone not unceasingly occupied with the Word of God must become corrupt; therefore we see what people in the higher schools are and grow up to be.... I greatly fear that schools for higher learning are wide gates to hell if they do not diligently teach the Holy Scriptures and

24

impress them on the young folk. [2]

John Calvin expressed similar views of education, as have subsequent Christian theologians. Obviously, however, it is not possible to implement these views of Christian education in the American public schools today.

First, America is a more pluralistic society than at the time of its founding. At that time nearly everyone held a Judeo-Christian world-view even though many may not have been Christians themselves. That is not true today. Now we have a multiplicity of sects and world-views, and those who hold non-Christian views have the same rights as Christians.

Second, the courts have interpreted the First Amendment so as to prohibit the public schools from teaching a comprehensive Christian world-view. The framers of the Bill of Rights intended the First Amendment to apply only to the federal government. But rightly or wrongly, the courts have implemented what they call the "incorporation doctrine." This holds that the "due process" clause of the Fourteenth Amendment incorporates most of the Bill of Rights, including the First Amendment, and makes it applicable to the states. Since school districts are state entities, the First Amendment is understood to prohibit the establishment of Christianity in the public schools.

The dilemma for the Christian teacher becomes apparent. He is faced with conflicting obligations. First, he has a duty to his Lord. The Christian teacher realizes that God has made all believers "ambassadors for Christ" to share the gospel of salvation with mankind. Surely, the Christian teacher rightly reasons, this includes an obligation to share Jesus Christ with the children in his classrooms during their most formative years.

At the same time, the Christian teacher has an obligation to his human superiors. This is not simply a human obligation. As already noted, the Scriptures command us to obey our employers and to work diligently for them. (See also I Timothy 6:1-2; Titus 2:9.) The school board hires teachers to teach certain subject matters, not to witness for Jesus Christ. Can a Christian math teacher fulfill his obligation to his earthly employer if he uses class time to talk about Jesus Christ instead of teaching math?

Then, the Christian teacher has a responsibility to the children in his classes. His duty to give them an outstanding academic education is obvious. And, at times, the teacher's judgment as to what is necessary for academic excellence differs from that of the principal, superintendent, or board because he also has a duty to give students a moral education. A teacher is a role model for his students. What he says and does, in and out of class, will be carefully observed and often imitated. But is it enough just to talk about good morals and to be a good example? Can the Christian teacher fulfill his entire obligation to his students if he does not tell them how they can have abundant life and eternal life through Christ?

The Christian teacher also has an obligation to the parents of the children in his class. The Bible strongly stresses the family as the basic governmental unit of society. God in His wisdom has placed children under the primary care and control of their parents (Psalm 127:3-5; Proverbs 4:1,10; Ephesians 6:1-4; Colossians 3:20; Exodus 20:12). The teacher should respect parental authority because it comes from God. And, the plain fact is, many parents do not want their children to be taught about Jesus Christ.

It may be difficult for the Christian teacher to understand the parent who does not want his child to learn about Christ, but God's institution, the family, is designed for believers and unbelievers alike. In civil society, the non-Christian parent has the same rights as the Christian parent. Imagine how you would feel if your child were taught in the public schools by an atheistic teacher who constantly tried to press his atheism on your child, or by a Jehovah's Witness who regularly shared Watchtower Society literature with his class. Our duty is to respect parental authority, recognizing that God in His providence has other ways of reaching those children with the gospel.

And yet, what about those children in the class who are Christians, and those who want to know Christ? Doesn't the Christian teacher have some sort of special obligation to them? And what of that substantial segment of society that wants some kind of Christian presence in the public schools? In a sense, the Christian teacher is their representative. In the arena of competing ideas which constitutes the public schools, he is their spokesman. Can he then go about his work and teach his classes just like any other teacher?

The opponents of Christianity use the public schools for their purposes. Secular Humanism is the movement that claims God is either nonexistent or irrelevant to modern man. It stresses that man is the measure of all things, the supreme value of the universe, and that no absolute God-given morals or values exist. It also declares that man is the chance product of an evolutionary process, that man has no soul or spirit, but is merely a complex animal who must solve his own problems through his own reason and technology. It is this force that permeates the educational system today and which has declared war upon Christianity. Secular Humanists have targeted the public schools as their primary battleground. As John Dumphy wrote in *The Humanist* magazine:

I am convinced that the battle for humankind's future must be waged and won in the public school classroom by teachers who correctly perceive their role as the proselytizers of a new faith: a religion of humanity that recognizes and respects the spark of what theologians call divinity in every human being. These teachers must embody the same selfless dedication as the most rabid fundamentalist preacher, for they will be ministers of another servant, utilizing a classroom instead of a pulpit to convey Humanist values in whatever subjects they teach regardless of the educational level—preschool day care or large state university. The classroom must and will become an arena of conflict between the old and the new—the rotting corpse of Christianity, together with all

*its adjacent evils and misery and the new faith of
Humanism resplendent in its promise of a world in which
the never realized Christian idea of "love thy neighbor"
will finally be achieved.* [3]

How do we resolve this dilemma? How does the Christian
teacher fulfill his duty to God and Caesar, to obey his Lord and
fulfill his duties to his superiors, his students and their parents
all at the same time? In a pluralistic society, how do we make
sure Christianity gets fair treatment while at the same time being
fair to the non-Christian?

On the one hand, we could try to implement Christian
education in the public schools. But this is unfair to non-
Christians and would never be allowed.

A second possibility is to teach "value free" education—just
stick with raw facts, and teach no morals or values whatsoever.
But technical knowledge without moral values is more
dangerous than ignorance, for man can use his reason to
become more beastly than any beast.

A third alternative is to teach basic moral values such as
honesty, loyalty, kindness, respect for human life, respect for
human dignity, et cetera, without reference to the religious
principles upon which those moral values are based. But this is
rather empty and incomplete. Invariably the questions must
arise: Why be honest? Why respect human life? What is the basis
for human dignity? The fact is that these values have their roots
in the Judeo-Christian tradition. We respect human dignity
because man is created in the image of God (Genesis 1:26). We
respect human life because God has commanded, "Thou shalt
not murder" (Exodus 20:13; Romans 13:9). We respect property
because God has said, "Thou shalt not steal" (Exodus 20:15;
Romans 13:9; Ephesians 4:28). We tell the truth because God
forbids us to bear false witness (Exodus 20:16; Romans 13:9). If
we are not allowed to assert the theistic, Judeo-Christian
tradition as the basis for our moral values, we are left with
ethical relativism and Secular Humanism. And, since the
Supreme Court has recognized Secular Humanism as a reli-

gion, [4] it is equally as unconstitutional to establish Secular Humanism as it is to establish Christianity.

The solution to this dilemma must be a combination of factors. First, the Christian teacher should strive for technical excellence in teaching. Christianity is never an excuse for shoddiness or mediocrity.

Second, the Christian teacher (and other teachers) should teach moral values. What moral values? That's a difficult question, but the best answer in our contemporary, pluralistic society appears to be those values that are commonly accepted by an overwhelming majority of that society. Fortunately, enough of the Judeo-Christian tradition remains in America that those moral values are, for the most part, Judeo-Christian moral values. The vast majority of Americans hold to those values even if they don't always practice them and even if they have lost sight of the Source of those values.

Third, teachers should not just teach moral values but should also show the basis for those values. Not all teachers will agree on these matters, so it is the special role of the Christian teacher to point to the Judeo-Christian tradition and the Bible that is its basis for contemporary American values. While some believe otherwise, it can be demonstrated easily that the Constitution and legal system of the United States, as well as most of Western Civilization, is based upon the Judeo-Christian tradition. [5] The role played by Christianity in American history, American sociology, and American politics deserves proper attention. The Biblical injunctions against abortion and premarital or extramarital sex are appropriate matters for comment. Thus, the Christian teacher should be free to talk about Christianity so long as it is relevant to the subject matter, so long as he does so in a factual rather than a "preaching" way, and so long as other teachers are free to share their views in the same manner.

Fourth, the Bible can be used as one source of moral lessons. U.S. Secretary of Education William Bennett, speaking on "Moral Literacy and the Formation of Character" at a Manhattan Institute gathering at the New York City Harvard Club in

November 1986, noted that children can learn loyalty from the book of Ruth, and kindness toward strangers from Christ's parable of the Good Samaritan. Dr. Bennett says knowing the "hard thoughts of Jeremiah and Jesus is surely part of moral literacy and it does not violate our Constitution." [6]

Fifth, in matters of worship and evangelism, the Christian teacher should have the same freedom other teachers have to share their views. Generally the principle of "equal access" should apply, especially before and after school. The Christian teacher should be a champion of the rights of Christian students to express their views in the public school arena.

Sixth, to the same extent that the Christian teacher is free to express his views and to encourage his Christian students to express their views, to that same extent he must respect the right of other teachers and students to express their views. If Christians are to have freedom of expression in the public arena, we must realize that other viewpoints which we may find highly disagreeable will be expressed there also. For that reason, the Christian parent who wants a thoroughly Christian education for his child will have to opt for private education or home education—and he should have that right. The Christian parent who chooses to send his child to the public school will have to accept the fact that his child will be exposed to anti-Christian ideas. But, likewise, the non-Christian parent who sends his child to the public schools will have to accept the fact that his child may be exposed to ideas he doesn't like—including Christianity.

Seventh, the Christian teacher always can and always should share Jesus Christ by his or her personal example. While the verbal message of Christ is necessary, so that the viewer will correlate the example with Him, there is much truth in the old saying, "I'd rather see a sermon than hear one any day."

Finally, no one can stop you from praying for your students, your fellow teachers, and your supervisors in your own home and in the privacy of your own soul.

FOOTNOTES

[1] *Catholic Encyclopedia*, "Education" (New York: The Gilmary Society, 1909, 1913), v:304.

[2] Martin Luther, *Luther's Works*, Weimar ed., VI: 461,462.

[3] John Dumphy, *The Humanist*, January/February 1982, p. 26.

[4] *Torcaso v. Watkins*, 367 U.S. 488 (1961).

[5] See generally Eidsmoe, *Christianity and the Constitution: Faith of Our Founding Fathers* (Grand Rapids: Baker Book House, 1987); Eidsmoe, *The Christian Legal Advisor* (Milford, Michigan: Mott Media, 1984; Grand Rapids: Baker Book House, 1987).

[6] U.S. Secretary of Education William Bennett, "Moral Literacy and the Formation of Character," lecture delivered at Manhattan Institute, New York City Harvard Club, November, 1986; quoted by John Chamberlain, "How to Teach Moral Literacy," *Tulsa Tribune*, December 23, 1986, p. 12-C.

Chapter 3

Tenure and Academic Freedom

Tenure is to the Christian teacher what Roman citizenship was to the Apostle Paul.

Paul did not hesitate to claim his Roman citizenship and use it as an avenue for the proclamation of the gospel. In Acts 16 we read that Paul and Silas had been beaten and cast into prison (vs. 23-24). The next morning the magistrates sent the sergeants to the prison to release Paul. When Paul was informed of his impending release, he said,

They have beaten us openly uncondemned, being Romans, and have cast us into prison; and now do they thrust us out privily? nay verily; but let them come themselves and fetch us out. And the sergeants told these words unto the magistrates: and they feared, when they heard that they were Romans. And they came and besought them, and brought them out, and desired them to depart from the city. (vs. 37-39)

Since it was unlawful to beat a Roman citizen, Paul received the "red carpet" treatment when the officials found out that he was a Roman citizen.

On another occasion Paul claimed his citizenship and his status as a Jew to gain the right to speak in Jerusalem. Paul was accused of having stirred up a riot in the city. The chief captain had him bound in chains and was having him carried to the jail. Paul asked to speak, and at first the chief captain refused. Then Paul said,

I am a man which am a Jew of Tarsus, a city in Cilicia, a citizen of no mean city: and, I beseech thee, suffer me to speak unto the people. And when he had given him license, Paul stood on the stairs, and beckoned with the hand unto the people. And when there was made a great silence, he spake unto them in the Hebrew tongue, saying . . . . (Acts 21:39-40)

Paul's citizenship and his status as a Jew secured for him the opportunity to share the gospel with a large audience. But when that audience turned against him, the chief captain wanted to scourge him with a whip. At this point Paul also claimed his Roman citizenship.

And as they bound him with thongs, Paul said unto the centurion that stood by, "Is it lawful for you to scourge a man that is a Roman, and uncondemned?" When the centurion heard that, he went and told the chief captain, saying, "Take heed what thou doest: for this man is a Roman." Then the chief captain came, and said unto him, "Tell me, art thou a Roman?" He said, "Yea." And the chief captain answered, "With a great sum obtained I this freedom." And Paul said, "But I was free born." Then straightway they departed from him which should have examined him: and the chief captain also was afraid, after he knew that he was a Roman, and because he had bound him. On the morrow, because he would have known the certainty wherefore he was accused of the Jews, he loosed him from his bands, and commanded the chief priests and all their council to appear, and brought Paul down, and set him before them. (Acts 22:25-30)

And when Paul stood before Festus, a governor who was politically beholden to the Jews (Acts 25:9), Paul again asserted his rights as a Roman citizen: "I appeal unto Caesar" (Acts 25:11). In accordance with Paul's demand, he was taken to Rome, where he ministered to the church at Rome for nearly three years.

Paul's special status as a Jew and as a Roman citizen gained him two things: (1) The right to speak freely about his beliefs;

and (2) The right to a fair hearing when accused of wrongdoing. This is essentially what tenure means to the Christian teacher.

What is Tenure?

A leading legal encyclopedia, *American Jurisprudence 2nd*, defines tenure as the "right to be employed indefinitely subject only to removal for certain enumerated causes and in a prescribed manner." [1] A more detailed description is found in the *Encyclopedia Dictionary of School Law:*

> *Tenure is a job security device. Tenure does not guarantee continual employment, but it does provide that a tenured teacher or administrator may not be removed from his or her position without specific or good cause. In addition, the school board is obligated to follow certain procedures in order to establish whether or not such cause exists.* [2]

There are good arguments for and against the concept of tenure. Proponents of tenure argue that it promotes academic freedom by giving teachers the liberty to express their views without fear of being fired for doing so, that it protects against being dismissed because of a personality conflict with an administrator or a principal who shows favoritism, and that it provides safeguards against a teacher being dismissed because of false and unfounded allegations.

Opponents contend that tenure prevents the firing of incompetent teachers, that it encourages tenured teachers to become lazy and apathetic since they have no fear of being fired, and that it allows teachers to create disharmony within a school system.

Thus a private school may legitimately choose to employ or not to employ tenure. Some private schools may stand for a distinctive doctrinal position and may not use tenure because tenure could prevent the school from dismissing teachers who do not share that position. Other private schools may choose to allow more diversity among their faculty, and they may choose to employ tenure as a means of guaranteeing job stability.

Since the public school is owned by all the people of the district, all persons should be free to express their viewpoints in it. The public school should not be under the exclusive control of a narrow element of society, whether Christian or non-Christian, conservative or liberal. For that reason tenure is generally desirable in a public institution.

How Tenure is Obtained

In most public elementary and secondary schools, tenure is semi-automatic. The teacher is considered to have tenure after a probationary period of several years. The exact number of years varies according to state law or state or local school board policy; three years is about average. In some jurisdictions, some form of evaluation might take place before the teacher is considered tenured.

In a college, the process of obtaining tenure is usually more complicated. In some colleges the administration has a screening process to evaluate the professor and to determine if he is fit for tenure. In most, a faculty committee votes on whether or not to grant tenure. This committee considers the professor's teaching skills, his academic and professional background, his student evaluations, his scholarly publications, his character, and other factors in making the tenure decision. The courts are divided on whether a tenure committee should be forced to reveal how its members voted. [3] In a case currently pending, a former professor at Bowling Green State University claims that he was denied tenure because of his creationist beliefs—even though he has excellent academic credentials, outstanding student evaluations, and more scholarly publications than the rest of his department combined! [4]

One reason the tenure decision is so serious, is that in many, if not most, universities a professor who has been denied tenure is given a terminal contract; that is, the following year at the university is his last. While this has the effect of eliminating unfit professors, it might also eliminate a professor who is highly qualified, or one who has great potential if certain deficiencies are corrected. One way to prevent this from happening is to have two committees—one to determine whether a professor should be granted tenure, and one to determine whether a professor who has been denied tenure should be continued in a non-tenured status.

Discharge for Cause

Theoretically at least, tenure is not the academic equivalent of eternal security—though sometimes it seems to work that way. Even a tenured teacher may be dismissed for cause.

So what constitutes good cause for dismissal? In some jurisdictions cause for dismissal of a tenured teacher is set forth in state statute. In others it may be specified in the teacher's contract. In others it may depend upon state or local school board regulations. All of these, of course, may be subject to the various constitutional protections discussed in Chapter One.

Here are several common grounds for dismissal:

(1) Incompetence is a valid reason for dismissal provided it can be proven. One case involving dismissal of a kindergarten teacher held that incompetence was not sufficiently proven when the only evidence was a visit to the classroom by a principal who had had no previous kindergarten experience. [5]

(2) Disloyalty toward the United States is also a valid reason. One of the principal functions of the public school system is to promote partriotism and good citizenship, and in this respect the teacher is a role model. [6]

(3) Immoral conduct is a valid reason to dismiss a tenured teacher. But what is immoral conduct? In a school context, one case defined immorality as "a course of conduct which offends the morals of a community and is a bad example to the youth whose ideals a teacher is supposed to foster and to elevate." [7] To what extent this includes sexual immorality is uncertain. Relevant considerations might include whether the sexual activity was purely private or whether it had become public knowledge (especially among the students), whether it was legal or illegal, whether there was an official school board policy

concerning such activity, and whether students or fellow teachers were involved.

(4) Insubordination is a valid ground, but mere criticism of officials is not insubordination. Insubordination must consist of disobedience of official directives, or spreading dissension or disharmony among students, teachers or staff. Admittedly, it is sometimes difficult to determine which is which. A word to the wise here: Be careful!

(5) What about violation of a dress code? A majority of cases seem to indicate that dress codes may be enforced, at least if they are reasonable and related to discipline or other school purposes. One Texas case held that a teacher could not be dismissed for growing a beard despite a school requirement that faculty be clean-shaven, [8] but another case held that a teacher could be fired for growing a beard. [9] (It may be significant that this teacher was not tenured.) A Connecticut case upheld the dismissal of a teacher for refusing to wear a necktie. A Massachusetts case upheld the dismissal of a teacher for wearing a miniskirt, [10] and another upheld the dismissal of a female principal for, among other things, appearing in public scantily clad. [11]

(6) A teacher may be dismissed for conviction of a criminal charge, but not just for having been charged with a crime. Nor may a teacher be dismissed for having refused to answer questions about a possible crime unless those questions concern disloyalty to the U.S. However, the school board may investigate the matter, make a determination as to whether or not the teacher did engage in criminal activity, and act accordingly. The school board need not wait until the teacher is convicted before dismissing him, and, in fact, the school board can determine that the teacher committed the illegal act and dismiss him even though he was acquitted in court. In order to do so, however, the school board must act upon good evidence.

(7) Gambling, at least if chronic or illegal, is a basis for dismissal.

(8) A teacher may be dismissed for intemperance. He might

successfully fight a dismissal if he had engaged only in moderate drinking; but if he were drunk, or if he used alcohol or other drugs illegally, or if he drank in the presence of students, the dismissal would probably be upheld.

(9) A teacher may be dismissed for financial unreliability, certainly if it involves school funds, and possibly in extreme cases of personal financial irresponsibility as well.

(10) A teacher may be dismissed for dishonesty or fraud, either personal or professional, whether in public or in private.

(11) All of the above presuppose some misconduct by the teacher. But what if, through no fault of the teacher, his services are no longer needed? That can be valid ground for dismissal also. Often this happens because of funding shortages, or because of declining enrollments, or because a school district has been reorganized. School district reorganizations or consolidations do not eliminate tenure rights, but if they result in a decline of faculty positions, even tenured teachers may be eliminated. In some jurisdictions, non-tenured teachers must be eliminated before tenured teachers, and in some jurisdictions, there are fixed rules as to which tenured teachers go first. In some districts, a tenured teacher who has been dismissed for this reason is entitled to first preference for a different position in the district or first preference for rehiring in the event a new position opens. [12] Of course, the reorganization or reduction in force must be done in good faith; if the teacher can show that his position was eliminated just to get rid of him, he could probably contest it successfully in court. [13]

(12) Some statutes and/or school board policies provide for dismissal for "other good and just cause." Such dismissals must be evaluated on a case-by-case basis.

Now, let's look at several items that do *not* constitute valid grounds for dismissal.

(1) The general rule is that one cannot be dismissed from a tenured public school teaching position for exercising First Amendment rights such as free speech, free press, freedom of

religion, et cetera. This includes the right to criticize school officials, even publicly and even in print, so long as it is done in a manner that is temperate and unlikely to interfere with school discipline and harmony. These First Amendment rights also include the right to engage in political activity. However, it is possible that school officials could prohibit political activity during school hours if they can show a valid reason for doing so.

(2) A teacher may not be dismissed for engaging in private employment, unless his teaching contract expressly prohibits such private employment or the private employment interferes with his work as a teacher.

(3) A teacher may not be dismissed for being married or having children. The only exception might be in school districts which have a policy prohibiting school employees from being married to each other. Even then, the school district would probably have to demonstrate a good reason for that policy.

(4) A tenured public school teacher probably may not be dismissed for sending his children to a private school. This has not been decided conclusively.

(5) A tenured teacher may not be dismissed for refusing to answer questions about a criminal offense pursuant to the Fifth Amendment. However, he may be dismissed for refusing to answer questions under oath about his loyalty to the United States.

(6) A tenured teacher may not be dismissed for residing outside the school district in which he is employed.

(7) At the present time, at least one case is pending to determine whether a teacher can be fired for refusing to join a union or teachers' association. [14] A federal statute, H.R. 4774, passed December 24, 1980, seems to afford some protection here. Section 19 provides that:

> *Any employee who is a member of and adheres to established and traditional tenets or teachings of a bona fide religion, body, or sect which has historically held conscientious objections to joining or financially sup- porting labor organizations shall not be required to join or*

39

financially support any labor organization as a condition of employment; except that such employee may be required in a contract between such employee's employer and a labor organization in lieu of periodic dues and initiation fees, to pay sums equal to such dues and initiation fees to a nonreligious, nonlabor-organization charitable fund exempt from taxation under section 501(c)(3) of title 26 of the Internal Revenue Code, chosen by such employee from a list of at least three such funds designated in such contract, or if the contract fails to designate such funds, then to any fund chosen by the employee. If such employee who holds conscientious objections pursuant to this section requests the labor organization to use the grievance-arbitration procedure on the employee's behalf, the labor organization is authorized to charge the employee for the reasonable cost of using such procedure.

In effect, this law gives the worker the right, as an alternative to paying dues to a union, to pay an equal amount to a charity instead, provided he is associated with a religious body that has conscientious objections to labor organizations. Assuming teachers' associations qualify as "labor organizations," this law could provide the teacher with the legal protection he needs.

(8) Can the tenured Christian teacher be fired for practicing his religion? Our view is that he cannot, provided he follows the guidelines in Chapter Four of this book.

What Else Can be Done to a Tenured Teacher?

As we have seen, tenure affords the teacher certain limited protection against dismissal without cause. But what other protection does tenure afford?

Recently, a Christian teacher approached one of the authors after a lecture. She had come under considerable fire for some conservative remarks she had made, and had been reassigned to another school in a district several miles away from her home and former school. She was convinced that her superiors had transferred her in order to pressure her to resign.

Did her tenure protect her? That's an open question. Tenure prevents the school board from demoting a teacher without cause. It does not, however, prevent the board from transferring a teacher to a different school even if this transfer works a substantial hardship on the teacher—unless it can be shown that the transfer was initiated as retaliation for the exercise of First Amendment freedoms. If she could prove that the superintendent reassigned her in retaliation for what she had said, she would have a good chance of overturning the transfer; otherwise, probably not.

Courts have held that tenure protects a principal from being demoted to teacher. But it does not protect a high school principal from being reassigned as a junior high school or elementary school principal, even though those positions may pay less than the high school position. Nor would it prohibit the superintendent from reassigning that principal from a large, prestigious high school to a small high school in the district, even though the transfer involved less prestige and less pay— provided the superintendent had a valid reason for the transfer. If the principal can show that he was transferred for impermissible reasons (retaliation against criticism, objections to having a Christian on the faculty, etc.), he probably has a good case to contest the action. The test is whether the superintendent and school board acted in good faith.

Procedural Guarantees

One aspect of tenure is the fact that a teacher may not be dismissed for expressing his views or for other improper reasons. The other aspect is the procedural protection which, in effect, guarantees a fair hearing to make sure no mistake has been made and that the action taken is appropriate.

What type of procedure is required for dismissal or other disciplinary action? It is not the same as a full court trial, but enough to guarantee fundamental fairness. The exact procedures are often specified in state law or in state or local regulations, but certain general principles apply.

First, the teacher is entitled to *notice*. He has a right to be informed in advance that he is to be dismissed. He has a right to be informed of the reasons for his proposed dismissal, in sufficient detail so that he is able to understand the reasons and defend against them if possible. Generally this notice will also include notice of his right to counsel, his right to a hearing, the date of the hearing, and so forth.

Second, the teacher is entitled to a *hearing*. Again, this is not a trial. Rather, it is an opportunity to be heard before a fact-finding body—possibly the school board, possibly another group—to determine whether the allegations against the teacher are true, and, if so, whether dismissal is the appropriate response. Normally the teacher is entitled to legal counsel at this hearing, though not necessarily at government expense. The teacher must be notified of the time, date, and place of the hearing sufficiently in advance so as to allow him adequate time to prepare a defense.

The board that holds the hearing must make its decisions based on hard evidence. The board probably need not follow the same precise rules of evidence that are used in the courts, but the evidence admitted must be competent. Under some circumstances, hearsay might be allowed at such a board meeting even though it would not be allowed in court, but the board must determine that it is reliable hearsay.

After the board has made its decision, the teacher normally has a right to *review*. This may be a review before another board, or the school board itself, or simply the right to appeal the decision to court. If a court were to determine that the school board had improperly dismissed the teacher, the court could order his reinstatement with back pay. However, the court would probably rule that the teacher had a duty to mitigate damages. That is, if the teacher was able to find similar work elsewhere between the time of his dismissal and the time of the court's decision, the salary he made or could have made at that position would be offset against the damage award from the school district.

The Rights of Non-Tenured Teachers

Constitutionally speaking, the rights of non-tenured teachers are considerably less than those of tenured teachers because of the Fourteenth Amendment. Part of the Fourteenth Amendment guarantees that "no state shall deprive any person of life, liberty or property without due process of law." Since tenure provides an expectation of continuing employment, the tenured teacher has a "property interest" in his teaching position. The state (i.e., the school board) cannot deprive him of that property interest without "due process of law"—that is, without just cause and fair procedures.

The non-tenured teacher does not have a property interest in continuing his job; he has little or no guarantee that his contract will be renewed. But he does have a right to continue his employment through the terms of his present contract—until June 1, for example—and the state cannot deprive him of that right without good cause and proper procedure.

In 1972 the U.S. Supreme Court ruled that a school board may not dismiss even a non-tenured teacher simply for exercising his First Amendment right to freedom of speech, or other constitutional rights. [15] But on the very same day, the Supreme Court also ruled that a non-tenured teacher is not entitled to procedural due process—a hearing, etc.—concerning his non-renewal. [16] In effect, the Supreme Court granted rights to non-tenured teachers in the first case, and then made it impractical for them to exercise those rights in the second! If a teacher can demonstrate to the court that he was fired for exercising his First Amendment freedoms, he will probably be successful in persuading the court to reinstate him and/or grant him monetary damages. But most of the time this will be difficult to prove. Everyone makes occasional mistakes that a hostile superintendent could latch on to and use as evidence for non-renewal. Since the superintendent and school board need not state the reasons for their decision not to rehire, it is difficult to prove in many cases.

While non-tenured teachers are somewhat lacking in constitutional protections, many states, state boards, or local or county boards of education have adopted policies giving non-tenured teachers procedural rights roughly equivalent to those of tenured teachers.

Academic Freedom

World Book Encyclopedia offers the following description of academic freedom:

> *For professors, academic freedom means the right to teach, to conduct research, and to write without fear of dismissal. For their students, it means the right to challenge the professors' views without being penalized. For the institutions, it means the right to determine what is taught and what research is conducted on campus. For [high school and elementary] teachers, such freedom means a greater share in selecting the contents of courses, and greater freedom to engage in political and social activities.* [17]

World Book suggests that the concept of academic freedom developed along with the rise of universities in Europe during the 1100s and 1200s. [18] In reality, the idea goes back at least as far as Plato's Academy in Greece nearly four centuries before Christ. Plato taught his scholars that their ultimate loyalty was not to Athens but to Truth, and that they must not allow political rulers to interfere with their search for Truth. [19]

During the twentieth century the American Association of University Professors (AAUP) and the Association of American Colleges (AAC) led a drive to expand academic freedom significantly. Owing largely to their efforts, academic freedom now includes certain rights for students, and certain rights for high school and elementary school teachers as well. Their efforts did not go unopposed, though. During a heated battle over academic freedom in 1916 the *New York Times* editorialized:

Academic freedom, that is, the inalienable right of every college instructor to make a fool of himself and his college by... intemperate, sensational prattle about every subject under heaven, to his classes and to the public, and still keep on the payroll or be reft therefrom only by elaborate process, is cried to all the winds by the organized dons. [20]

Even today the concept of academic freedom does not meet with universal acceptance. Its supporters argue that it encourages free inquiry which leads to truth, and that it prevents discrimination. Opponents contend that it promotes disharmony and allows professors to undermine the very institutions that provide their livelihood. The AAC's Committee on Academic Freedom and Tenure of Office stated in 1917:

A man who accepts a position in a college which he has reason to believe is a Christian institution and who, further, may properly infer that the canons of good taste forbid, perhaps, the asking when the contract is made, of intimate personal questions about his own religious belief, can scarcely assume that freedom of speech includes either the right privately to undermine or publicly to attack Christianity. The man called to the average college which believes in monogamy as essential in the upbuilding of student character can scarcely expect the college to submit to a long judicial process in tardily effecting his release if he openly states and on inquiry admits that he believes in free love.

Incompatability of temperament in an educational institution is as serious a problem as in marriage; and since no right-minded corporation will make a contract for life with a new teacher, divorce in a college would seem to be open to few objections provided it be done decently and in order. [21]

The crusade for academic freedom led to the adoption of the 1940 statement of the Association of American Colleges, which is among the most noteworthy statements of the meaning of

45

academic freedom:

The purpose of this statement is to promote public understanding and support of academic freedom and tenure and agreement upon procedures to assure them in colleges and universities. Institutions of higher education are conducted for the common good and not to further the interest of either the individual teacher or the institution as a whole. The common good depends upon the free search for truth and its free exposition.

Academic freedom is essential to these purposes and applies to both teaching and research. Freedom in research is fundamental to the advancement of truth. Academic freedom in its teaching aspect is fundamental for the protection of the rights of the teacher in teaching and of the student to freedom in learning. It carries with it duties correlative with rights.

Tenure is a means to certain ends; specifically: (1) Freedom of teaching and research and of extramural activities, and (2) A sufficient degree of economic security to make the profession attractive to men and women of ability. Freedom and economic security, hence tenure, are indispensable to the success of an institution in fulfilling its obligations to its students and to society.

ACADEMIC FREEDOM

(a) The teacher is entitled to full freedom in research and in the publication of the results, subject to the adequate performance of his other academic duties; but research for pecuniary return should be based upon an understanding with the authorities of the institution.

(b) The teacher is entitled to freedom in the classroom in discussing his subject, but he should be careful not to introduce into his teaching controversial matter which has no relation to his subject. Limitations of academic freedom because of religious or other aims of the institution should be clearly stated in writing at the time of the appointment.

(c) The college or university teacher is a citizen, a member of a learned profession, and an officer of an educational institution. When he speaks or writes as a citizen, he should be free from institutional censorship or discipline, but his special position in the community imposes special obligations. As a man of learning and an educational officer, he should remember that the public may judge his profession and his institution by his utterances. Hence he should at all times be accurate, should exercise appropriate restraint, should show respect for the opinions of others, and should make every effort to indicate that he is not an institutional spokesman.

ACADEMIC TENURE

(a) After the expiration of a probationary period, teachers or investigators should have permanent or continuous tenure, and their services should be terminated only for adequate cause, except in the case of retirement for age, or under extraordinary circumstances because of financial exigencies.

In the interpretation of this principle it is understood that the following represents acceptable academic practice:

(1) The precise terms and conditions of every appointment should be stated in writing and be in the possession of both institution and teacher before the appointment is consummated.

(2) Beginning with appointment to the rank of full-time instructor or a higher rank, the probationary period should not exceed seven years, including within this period full-time service in all institutions of higher education; but subject to the proviso that when, after a term of probationary service of more than three years in one or more institutions, a teacher is called to another institution it may be agreed in writing that his new appointment is for a probationary period of not more than four years, even though thereby the person's total probationary period in

the academic profession is extended beyond the normal maximum of seven years. Notice should be given at least one year prior to the expiration of the probationary period if the teacher is not to be continued in service after the expiration of that period.

(3) During the probationary period a teacher should have the academic freedom that all other members of the faculty have.

(4) Termination for cause of a continuous appointment, or the dismissal for cause of a teacher previous to the expiration of a term appointment, should, if possible, be considered by both a faculty committee and the governing board of the institution. In all cases where the facts are in dispute, the accused teacher should be informed before the hearing in writing of the charges against him and should have the opportunity to be heard in his own defense by all bodies that pass judgment upon his case. He should be permitted to have with him an adviser of his own choosing who may act as counsel. There should be a full stenographic record of the hearing available to the parties concerned. In the hearing of charges of incompetence, the testimony should include that of teachers and other scholars, either from his own or from other institutions. Teachers on continuous appointment who are dismissed for reasons not involving moral turpitude should receive their salaries for at least a year from the date of notification of dismissal whether or not they are continued in their duties at the institution.

(5) Termination of a continuous appointment because of financial exigency should be demonstrably bona fide. [22]

Academic freedom may be applied differently in a private school or college than in a public institution. A private school is founded and supported by individuals or groups, and they have a right to expect that their school, its staff and the faculty will stand for certain principles. Some private schools choose to allow free inquiry in a manner very similar to that of public schools. Others choose to take a distinct doctrinal stand and require their faculty to conform thereto or teach elsewhere. Both are legitimate forms of education, and a free and diverse society should encourage the development of both.

But in a public institution, academic freedom helps to ensure that all segments of society have a voice in the public schools, since all segments of society own, support, and use them.

Even in a public university, academic freedom has its limits. The university should have every right to fire a teacher who advocates the violent overthrow of the United States, or who urges his students to engage in an illegal or harmful activity such as drug abuse. Whether a state university should be allowed to fire a professor for advocating free love or a homosexual lifestyle is a closer question. An argument could be made that the family is a basic unit of society and essential for social stability, that homosexuality and free love undermine the family, and therefore society has a right to expect its public universities to promote family stability and discourage homosexuality and free love.

At the high school and elementary school levels, academic freedom is more limited. In fact, until about the 1960s it was commonly thought that academic freedom applied only to higher education. That has changed, but only partially. In a sense, the public school stands *in loco parentis*, in place of the parent. Those who attend universities are for the most part adults, legally speaking at least. Those who attend elementary and high schools are children. The parents of those children have a right to expect that certain values will be conveyed to them, and that they will receive decent moral training as well as academic training. Their minds are more impressionable than those of college students. And, of course, the minds of elementary school children are more impressionable than those of high school students. In general, the younger children are, the less capable they are of distinguishing fact from opinion. As a result, the younger the children are, the more limited academic freedom for the teacher becomes.

It is fair to say that public elementary and secondary schools may expect their teachers to uphold, or at least not to undermine, certain basic values adhered to by a vast majority of the population, values that are essential to the preservation of the nation. These would include the following principles:

(1) That Americans should love and serve their country (though this would not mean our nation should never be criticized, nor should a teacher be fired for advocating pacifism).

(2) That laws are to be obeyed (though one could argue that there are legitimate cases of civil disobedience).

(3) That freedom is better than tyranny, that representative government is better than authoritarianism, and that limited republican government is better than totalitarianism.

(4) That the principles of American government as embodied in our organic laws, the Declaration of Independence and the Constitution, are to be upheld as true and as in the best interest of our nation.

(5) That diligence, excellence, thrift and hard work are beneficial both for the individual and for society.

(6) That cleanliness, personal hygiene, and good health practices promote a better quality of life.

(7) That our environment and natural resources are to be used carefully.

(8) That courtesy, kindness and respect for the rights of others is desirable.

(9) That honesty is the best policy.

(10) That the family (including parental authority) is a basic unit for the well-being of the individual and society, and that practices which undermine the family are to be discouraged.

Within that framework of values, the public school teacher should have substantial freedom to express his views, so long as such expression does not take place in a dogmatic and authoritarian manner and does not detract substantially from the teaching of the basic subject matter.

It will be noted that belief in God or Christianity was not listed among the ten basic values shown above. These beliefs were not included because of the way the U.S. Supreme Court has interpreted the establishment clause in cases such as *Torcaso v. Watkins* and others. [23] A strong case could be made, however, that the ten values listed above are dependent upon a basic underlying belief in God, and that these values cannot be sustained over a long period of time if that belief in God is removed.

At the very least, the Christian teacher should have the same academic freedom to express his belief in God that other teachers have to express their views. If they are not allowed to do so, the result is "practical atheism," a thought-system that, while not necessarily expressly denying God, treats Him as though He doesn't exist.

A strong argument can be made that Christians, especially conservative evangelicals, are the most discriminated-against minority (if, in fact, they are a minority) in America today. In many modern universities, Christianity is virtually the *only* belief system that is not considered socially and academically acceptable.

In practice, many of these universities are not as open-minded as they claim to be. Dominated by liberals, they are open to many forms of thought, but very closed-minded toward conservative Christianity. *HIS* magazine reported:

> *James Q. Wilson, the eminent student of American government and politics, once remarked that he had spent much of his life confined within authoritarian institutions—the Catholic Church when he was a child, the United States Navy when he was a young man, Harvard University as a tenured professor. As a totalitarian system demanding conformity of thought the greatest of these, he said, was Harvard.* [24]

Nowhere is the hostility and hypocrisy of the academic community more apparent—or transparent—than in its attitude toward creation science. Even though there are thousands of degreed scientists who hold the creationist position, even though there is a growing body of scientific literature defending creationism, even though much evidence supports creationism, and even though the evolutionary model has many flaws and unanswered questions, creation science remains an unthinkable anathema on many college campuses. Creationist professors have been denied tenure; doctoral dissertations of creationist candidates have been rejected; creationist applicants for graduate programs have been turned down, and creationist term papers have been given Fs—all by professors who in any other context would defend to the death the right of academic freedom.

At Iowa State University in 1983, a student was dismissed from class for having complained about the professor's dogmatic teaching of evolution. (The university reinstated the student.) The professor expressed amazement that students who have publicly rejected biological evolution and who believe the universe is only 10,000 years old are nevertheless allowed to pass science courses and graduate from the university. He declared,

> *I suggest that every professor should reserve the right to fail any student in his class, no matter what the grade record indicates, whenever basic misunderstandings of a certain magnitude are discovered. Moreover, I would propose retracting grades and possibly even degrees if such gross misunderstandings are publicly espoused after passing the course or after being graduated.* [25]

The professor later insisted that his remarks did not amount to condemning students for their beliefs, but his statement speaks for itself. Such bigotry would be downright comical were it not for its tragic consequences for the students and professors involved and for the fact that it makes a sham of academic freedom.

True academic freedom contains room for wide areas of diversity. Certainly it is broad enough to make room for Judeo-Christian thought.

FOOTNOTES

[1] *American Jurisprudence 2d* Vol. 68, "Schools" Section 149.

[2] Richard D. Gatti and Daniel J. Gatti, ed., *Encyclopedia Dictionary of School Law* (West Ynack, New York: Parker Publishing Co., 1975), p. 287.

[3] *Balubergs v. Board of Regents of the University System of Georgia, In re Dinnan,* 661 F.2d 426 (5th Cir. 1981), cert. den. 50 U.S.L.W. 3963 (June 7, 1982) (holding that a tenure vote must be revealed); *Gray v. Board of Higher Education,* 92 F.R.D. 87, 27 F.E.P. 256 (F.D.N.Y. 1981) (holding that a tenure vote is privileged and must be kept confidential).

[4] Jerry Bergman, *The Criterion: Religious Discrimination in America* (Richfield, Minnesota: Onesimus Publishing, 1984).

[5] For all of these grounds for dismissal see general *American Jurisprudence 2d,* (AmJur2d), Vol. 68, "Schools," Section 149-180. Many case citations are contained therein.

[6] Ibid.

[7] *Horosko v. School District of Mt. Pleasant.* 335 Penn. 369, 6 A.2d 866, cert. den. 308 U.S. 553.

[8] *Hander v. San Jacinto Junior College,* 519 F.2d 273 (Texas).

[9] *Ball v. Board of Trustees,* 584 F.2d. 684.n).

[10] *Tardif v. Quinn,* 545 F.2d 761 (Massachusetts) (miniskirt); *East Hartford Education Association v. Board of Education,* 562 F.2d 838 (Connecticut) (necktie).

[11] *McCutcheon v. Board of Education,* 419 N.E.2d 451 (Illinois, 1981).

[12] *McMullen v. District School Board,* 533 P.2d 812.

[13] *Perry v. Sinderman,* 408 U.S. 593 (1972); see also *Mt. Healthy City School District Board of Education v. Doyle,* 50 L.Ed.2d 471, 97 S.Ct. 568.

[14] *Board of Regents v. Roth,* 408 U.S. 564 (1972).

[15] *World Book Encyclopedia,* 1985 ed., "Academic Freedom," A. Harry Passow, I: 16-17.

[16] Ibid.

[17] Russell Kirk, *Academic Freedom: An Essay in Definition* (Chicago: Henry Regnery Company, 1955), pp. 11-13.

[18] "The Professors' Union," *New York Times* editorial quoted in *School and Society,* III (January 29, 1916), p. 175.

[19] "Report," Committee on Academic Freedom and Tenure of Office, Bulletin, Association of American Colleges, III (April, 1917), p. 51.

[20] 1940 Statement on Academic Freedom by Association of American Colleges; pp. 487-489.

[21] *Torcaso v. Watkins,* 367 U.S. 488 (1961).

[22] Lewis H. Lapham, *Harper's*; quoted in "Media Mind," *HIS* Magazine, March 1982, p. 21.

[23] "Competence and Controversy: Issues and Ethics on the University/Psuedoscience Battlefield," *The Skeptical Inquirer,* Fall 1983 (Vol. 8), pp. 2-5.

Chapter 4

Sharing Christ in the Classroom

• In New Jersey, Marie Russo, a biology teacher, sponsored a Christian concert and told Christian students about it. The concert was off campus and not during school hours, but 70-80 students attended. She also told her students about the Equal Access Act, which provides for the use of public school buildings for religious activities outside school hours, and she made New Testaments available at Christmas. For these actions, she was cut to a part-time position. She was called to a school board meeting and told she could not mention God, deity, or Jesus in or out of the schoolroom, because to do so would violate separation of church and state. She was asked to sign a statement of understanding which outlined that she could teach humanism but that she could not teach about God.

Was the teacher within her rights? Should she have signed the statement? What would you have done?

• In a junior high school in North Carolina, teachers were commonly allowed to read whatever they wished on lunch duty. Linda Ellis, a math teacher, chose to read her Bible. Her principal issued her a letter of reprimand directing her not to read her Bible while on school property and forbidding her from discussing religious questions, even those initiated by students, on school property. Later, she was denied a new contract.

Does the Constitution allow Linda Ellis to read her Bible during lunch duty? Did the school principal violate her constitutional rights?

• Teachers in a Tennessee elementary school routinely join

the National Education Association and its local affiliates. One teacher, Herman Partin, had a 12-year unblemished record as a teacher, and for those 12 years he had belonged to the NEA. But, as a Christian, he finally decided he couldn't support the pro-abortion position of the NEA, so he refused to renew his membership. The principal tried to deny Partin the pay raise to which he was entitled under a new state program for veteran teachers, giving as an additional reason the fact that Partin was "one of those fanatical Christians who believe Jesus Christ is the only way to heaven."

Does a teacher who takes Jesus' words (John 14:6) according to their plain meaning have a place in the public schools? Was Herman Partin entitled to his pay raise despite the fact that he resisted compulsory unionism?

Each of these cases was resolved out of court. Thanks to the capable intervention of Michael Farris of Concerned Women for America, Marie Russo was restored to her full-time position and was given back pay and tenure. Attorney Carl Horn assisted Linda Ellis and secured not only her right to read her Bible at lunch but also a 16-point policy concerning religious freedom for public school teachers. The Rutherford Institute represented Herman Partin and secured for him his raise; however, he had to accept a transfer to another school. [1] But in each of these cases, it is unclear what would have happened if the case had gone through the courts.

In the preceding chapters we've talked in general terms about the legal and constitutional rights of teachers. Now let's get down to specifics. What can and can't a Christian teacher do to witness for his faith, inside or outside the classroom?

First, some basic considerations should be noted.

(1) A teacher does have a dual role. On the one hand, you are a citizen with First Amendment rights. On the other hand, you are an agent of the state. To the extent your Christian witness reflects your beliefs and actions as an individual citizen, it is likely to be upheld. To the extent it appears to be an official

position of the state, it is likely to be struck down as unconstitutional.

(2) The First Amendment is a two-edged sword. What you are allowed to do depends, in part, upon what others are allowed to do. If others, whose convictions may be very different from yours, are allowed to express themselves, your right to express yourself is more likely to be upheld. This is the "public forum" concept discussed in Chapter One. If the school system allows teachers a general freedom to express their ideas, the school system cannot discriminate against your views just because they are religious.

(3) School board policies are relevant here. You might say there are three categories: (a) That which the school board *must* allow you to say and do because of the free speech clause and the free exercise clause (such as, having a Bible on your desk); (b) That which the school board *must not* allow you to do because of the establishment clause (such as, leading your students in the Lutheran liturgy during class); and (c) That which the school board *in its discretion* may or may not choose to allow you to do.

(4) Community attitudes may also make a difference. Even though this may not be relevant for constitutional or legal purposes, a Christian witness is much more likely to be allowed if you have general community approval.

(5) If your witness is relevant to the subject matter, it is much more likely to be upheld than if it is not. For example, a discussion of the Christian view of sex and marriage may be permissible in a health class, but probably not in a math class.

(6) The older your students are, the more freedom you have to share your ideas with them. The reason is that older students are more likely to be able to distinguish your personal views from the official position of the state.

(7) Tenure strengthens your case. While a non-tenured teacher has First Amendment rights, it is much more difficult for him to assert them.

(8) There is a time to assert your rights and a time not to do so. You can fight for your right to witness and perhaps win, but in the process you might offend many people and drive them away from the Lord. If so, you may win a battle but lose the war. Whether to stand for your rights or to give in is a difficult decision that must be made with much thought, soul-searching, and prayer.

Now let's look at some specific areas of concern.

School Prayer

In 1962 the U.S. Supreme Court ruled that "it is not the business of government to compose official prayers for any group of the American people to recite as a part of a religious program carried on by government (*Engel v. Vitale*)." [2] The prayer in question was a nonsectarian prayer which simply declared, "Almighty God, we acknowledge our dependence upon Thee, and we beg Thy blessings upon us, our parents, our teachers and our country." No child was required to say the prayer, and any child could leave the room during the prayer if he or his parents desired. Nevertheless, the Court ruled that such a prayer was an establishment of religion.

While the prayer in *Engel* was an official prayer composed by the school system, the same principle would probably apply to a prayer composed by an individual teacher for the use of his class, or a prayer selected from some source, such as the Lord's Prayer or the Twenty-Third Psalm. Organized prayer sessions conducted as part of class appear to be forbidden.

However, silent prayer or meditation is probably permissible. In *Wallace v. Jaffree* the U.S. Supreme Court upheld a 1978 Alabama statute calling for a moment of silence, but it struck down a 1981 amendment which called for spoken prayer and which set forth the purpose of the moment of silence as being "for meditation or silent prayer." The Court noted that the state senator who sponsored the 1981 amendment called it an "effort to return voluntary prayer to our public schools" and said it was "a beginning and a step in the right direction." The Court therefore concluded that the purpose of the amendment was clearly religious and therefore unconstitutional.

The *Jaffree* decision may be faulted on several grounds, particularly its over-reliance upon the statement of one senator as to legislative purpose. But the decision does allow silent meditation provided the law or policy is carefully drawn so as to avoid the appearance of promoting religion. The fact that a statute expressly mentions prayer as one option available to the student would probably not be sufficient to constitute an establishment of religion if the legislative history were not as blatant as in the *Jaffree* case. A New Jersey statute allowing silent prayer or meditation is currently being considered in the courts and may provide more definitive guidance in this area.

Neither *Engel* nor *Jaffree* in any way prohibits a teacher or student from praying on his own, either privately or publicly. Bonnie Berggren, a former public school teacher and now a college librarian, writes:

> As a home economics teacher, I often ate meals with my students. I continued to bow my head in silent prayer, which I had always done before meals. Often the students followed my lead. I prayed with a student in the hall one day when I found her crying over her hospitalized mother. We later discussed prayer as an option during a problem-solving unit. [3]

The Christian teacher needs to use this privilege of prayer with discretion, but it is a very powerful weapon which even the Supreme Court cannot take away.

Equal Access

In August 1984 Congress passed the Equal Access Act, and President Reagan signed it into law. The concept of equal access had been around for a long time before passage of the Act, and many believe equal access to public facilities is a constitutional right whether set forth in statute or not. On the other hand, those who believe in a radical separation of church and state believe the Equal Access Act is an unconstitutional violation of the establishment clause of the First Amendment.

In *Vincent v. Widmar* [4] the Supreme Court upheld the concept of equal access as applied to Christian groups meeting on state university campuses, but the Court has not yet ruled on the application of equal access to public high schools or elementary schools. Many had hoped the Court would decide the issue in the 1986 *Bender v. Williamsport* case, [5] and in that case the Court did give a strong indication that the concept will eventually be upheld. Four justices voted to uphold the right of Christian students to meet in public schools; but five justices ruled that the issue in that case was "moot" because the school board member who had originally challenged the Christian group's right to meet was no longer on the school board by the time the case came to the Supreme Court. An Omaha, Nebraska case currently making its way through the courts may ultimately provide the landmark ruling necessary.

The Equal Access Act provides that public schools must allow student initiated religious groups to use school facilities for their activities before and after regular classroom instruction hours. There are three qualifications for this use: (1) The school must receive federal funds, which nearly all do in some form or another. (2) The school must be a "public forum." That is, it must be open for the free expression of ideas. Unless the school completely bans any and all extracurricular activities, it will probably be considered a public forum. (3) The Act applies only to secondary schools. This does not mean elementary schools are prohibited from allowing student groups to meet, but the Act does not require them to do so.

In effect, then, the Equal Access Act means that if public schools allow some noncurriculum-related student groups to use school facilities, they may not refuse religious groups the right to meet. The Act simply prohibits the public schools from discriminating against religious groups and treating religious students as second-class citizens. If the Chess Club or the Shakespearian Society, Young Democrats or Young Republicans are allowed to meet on campus, so may Youth for Christ.

Religious groups have the same right to meet in school facilities as other groups, no more and no less.

The Equal Access Act is, though, limited to students. The Act does not confer upon outside persons a right to come on campus and speak to students or organize them into groups. School officials are free to open their facilities to outside persons, but they are not required to do so.

To come under the protection of the Equal Access Act, the student group must be student initiated and student led. That is, it must be a student sponsored, not a state sponsored, activity. According to Section 802(f) and Section 803(2), the assignment of a teacher, administrator or other school employee to a meeting for custodial purposes does not constitute sponsorship of a meeting.

Does this mean a teacher may not organize a Christian group? Does it mean student groups may not meet during school hours? Not at all. It simply means the Equal Access Act does not require the school to permit such activity. So long as the school officials allow you to do so, you are free to go beyond the Equal Access Act, subject only to the limitations of the establishment clause of the First Amendment.

The Christian teacher may wish to work closely with Christian student groups, offering them such assistance, counsel and encouragement as school officials will allow. If school policy requires that a teacher be assigned to monitor such groups, you might wish to volunteer for that assignment.

Released Time

Released time programs exist in many states and school districts. They provide that public school children may be released from school for a certain time period each week, usually several hours, to attend religious instruction by their respective churches.

In 1948 the Supreme Court struck down a released time provision in *McCollum v. Board of Education;* [6] but in 1952, the court upheld a released time provision in *Zorach v. Clauson.* [7] The main difference is that the released time provision in *McCollum* involved religious instruction in public school classrooms by church ministers coming on campus with school personnel arranging the rooms, etc. In *Zorach* the students were released from school and went to their respective churches to attend the instruction there. Thus, in *Zorach* the appearance of state-sponsorship was considerably lessened. While the *McCollum* situation was considered an *establishment* of religion, the *Zorach* program was considered an *accommodation* of religion which is permissible.

As a public school teacher, your personal involvement in any released time program will be minimal. But you might check whether your state law provides for released time or whether local school board policy contains such a provision. If so, and if students in your school wish to be released for religious instruction, you might be their spokesman to make sure their right to released time is protected.

The Bible and the Public Schools

In the 1963 case of *Abington Township v. Schempp,* [8] the Supreme Court invalidated as an establishment of religion a Pennsylvania statute which required that at least ten verses from the Holy Bible be read without comment at the opening of each public school day even though children whose parents objected to the reading could be excused from class. The Court reasoned that the reading of the Bible in that manner constituted an act of worship and an entanglement of government with religion.

Horace Mann, whom some regard as the father of the public schools, would have been shocked by this decision. Even though Mann was a Unitarian, he declared in an 1844 letter that he wanted the Bible used in the public schools because it "makes known to us the rule of life and the means of salvation." [9] Mann wanted to free the public schools from local denominational control but not from Christian influence. He emphasized that " ... our system earnestly inculcates all

Christian morals; it founds its morals on the basis of religion; it welcomes the religion of the Bible, it allows it to do what it is allowed to do in no other system, to speak for itself." [10]

But the *Schempp* decision did not totally ban the Bible from the public schools. In fact, the Court emphasized that, "Nothing we have said here indicates that such study of the Bible or of religion, when presented objectively as part of a secular program of education, may not be effected consistent with the First Amendment."

The use of the Bible is permitted in the public schools so long as it is (1) presented objectively, and (2) used for secular educational purposes.

But this approach presents problems. Evangelical Christians regard the Bible as the inspired and infallible Word of God. Many argue that treating the Bible merely as literature demeans it and leads to a loss of faith. Treating the Bible as literature and subjecting it to literary criticism as one would any other literary work, in their view, is worse than not using the Bible at all.

And, much of what passes for "objective" study of the Bible is not objective at all. Rather, it presents a biased liberal view of Scripture and theology. One textbook commonly used in public schools is *Adventures in World Literature*. This text contains a section titled "Sumerian and Hebrew Literatures," placing Sumerian mythology beside the Bible as though the two were equals. After "The Epic of Gilgamesh" (the Sumerian flood narrative), the book contains the Genesis account of creation, part of which is titled "The Story of Eden" (note the term "story" instead of "account"). At the end is an editors' comment:

> *Genesis was not the work of an individual. From studying textual differences, Bible scholars have agreed that "Creation" (Genesis 1) and "The Story of Eden" (Genesis 2), for example, show the work of two different authors.* [11]

In this way the author not only expresses his view that Genesis was not solely the work of Moses, but rather was the work of more than one author. This is the liberal view of higher criticism most popularly embodied in the Graf-Wellhausen theory, or JEDP theory, or documentary hypothesis. The author goes further by implying that "Bible scholars have agreed" that this is the case, thus insinuating that anyone who does not agree is, by definition, not a Bible scholar. This is simply untrue.

Treating the Bible objectively, then, can mean treating it as though it is merely the work of men, replete with errors and myths. But does it *have* to be that way? Can the Bible be presented to public school students in a manner that does not offend the Constitution, and one that is acceptable to evangelical Christians?

Dr. Joyce L. Vedral, an English teacher in a New York City high school, taught a course on the Bible as literature. She explained her basis for teaching the course:

The Bible has influenced English literature more than any other book in the language. Without familiarity with the Bible, students hoping to go to college suffer a great disadvantage. Since few people in their teens (unfortunately) go to church on a regular basis, they have little or no knowledge of the Bible. For this reason, English departments are more than delighted to introduce courses in the Bible as literature.

On that basis she "sold" the course to school officials. But then she had to sell the course to students.

Who would sign up for "Bible" if they saw it written on a paper? They would think it was either boring or "religious." So I determined to go around and recruit students.

It was surprisingly easy. All I had to do was to appeal to their natural curiosity and to their sense of adventure. I gave a ten-minute speech in each of the English classes, announcing my name and the course I wanted to begin. I then plunged into questions such as: "Have you ever wondered who created God, or how everything started if there is no God? Is there a devil? Who created him (it)? What does the Bible say about witchcraft? What does the Bible say happens after death? Do you agree with the Bible? Do you know that Jesus never said a word about sex before marriage?"

At this point the class would be in an uproar. All kinds of questions were hurled my way, and the teacher in charge of the class would try to restore order. "Calm down," I would say. "I can't deal with all of your questions now. You'll have to sign up for the course. At that time you'll have an opportunity to ask any question you want, and to express your own opinion on any issue you want. After we read the Bible, you can agree or disagree with it, and then you will have a chance to debate with priests, rabbis and ministers. They will come to the class and give their 'rap,' and after listening respectfully, you'll have a chance to question anything they say. Yes, to ask those questions you could never ask in church or temple in the middle of a sermon."

I added, "In addition to all this, you will be reading the most quoted book in English literature, and you will greatly increase your insight into English literature. Also, it doesn't look half bad on a college transcript, if you've taken 'Bible as Literature.' "

After three days of recruiting, I had 500 students signed up.

But how did she teach the course? She rarely took a stand on issues herself. Rather, she brought in outside speakers to do that. She describes her teaching:

I never tell the students that a particular miracle or doctrine is "true." Rather I discuss the biblical passage and ask for opinions. Then, at times, I give my opinion, adding that even I cannot prove it and that I base my opinion on many factors, faith included. The students love this approach because it frees them to think for themselves without guilt. . . .

In the course we read the Bible stories to find the "principle" or "teaching" and discuss whether or not the individuals in the class agree with the principle.

For example, a study of the story of Jacob and Esau demonstrates the principle of "reaping and sowing" or, "What goes around comes around" as the students reinterpret it. What you do comes back to you in the long run. Jacob deceived his brother Esau into selling him the birthright, and Jacob is later deceived by his father-in-law Laban, who tricks him into marrying Leah, the wrong wife.

The class tosses it around. Do they agree? Most of them seem to find evidence in their own lives that what they do usually has repercussions.

We discuss the life of Abraham which demonstrates the principle of faith. We delve into the life of Joseph and analyze the element of a "call" or a "destiny," discussing Joseph's dreams.

Students volunteer stories of personal experiences involving faith or destiny or reaping and sowing. Judy tells how she got a job by faith. Paul tells how he knows he will be a famous soccer player. [12]

The Christian teacher who desires to share the Bible with his students might try to initiate such a course in his school. Several texts are available. *The Bible as Literature* (Webster/McGraw-Hill, New York) divides the Bible for study by literary form. Zondervan of Grand Rapids publishes Leland Ryken's *The Literature of the Bible*. It is intended for college audiences but could be a good teacher's resource. Mott Media of Milford, Michigan has published some shorter books on Bible literature themes: *Heroes of Genesis, The Epic of the Exodus, Parables and Portraits of the Bible, Poetry of the Bible, The Garden and the City,* and *Heroines of the Bible.*

Rather than having a special course on the Bible *as* literature, the teacher may choose to have a general course on world literature and include excerpts from the Bible as part of the course. Or the teacher might have a course, or part of a course, on the Bible *in* literature, considering what use Shakespeare made of the Bible, etc. The textbook *The Bible as/in Literature* (Scott, Foresman & Co., Chicago) might be a valuable asset for one of these courses. [13]

Still another possibility is a course on comparative religions. In the hands of the right teacher, and with the aid of the Holy Spirit, such courses could be helpful in stimulating religious interest and leading students to a closer relationship with God. Certainly such a course could be dangerous since it could easily lead to the conclusion that all religions are of equal value as ways of coming to God. But a capable teacher could, through eliciting student response, show clearly how Christianity differs from all other religions in that it is based upon the reality of an historical Person who offers salvation, not by works, but by the free gift of grace through faith. At the very least, such a course could make the way of salvation through Christ clear to all who want to know Him.

Furthermore, the Bible may be used in any course where its message is relevant to the subject matter. Any course on ancient history would be incomplete without reference to the Bible as a sourcebook, for the Bible is the basic history of the Jewish people and other peoples, and the Jews were and are one of the most influential peoples in world history. The effect of Christianity upon the Roman Empire, or upon the Middle Ages, or upon the Crusades, or upon early American history is certainly a proper subject for class lecture and discussion. At the time of this writing, as a result of two cases involving the teaching of secular humanism in Tennessee and Alabama, several textbook publishers have acknowledged that their treatment of religion has been shoddy in the past and have announced steps to provide more balanced and complete treatment of religion in future editions.

One of the best ways a teacher can witness for the Lord is to have a Bible on his desk. The Bible is universally recognized as a religious symbol, and its very presence says something about your attitude toward it and toward God. Not only that, it is a great conversation starter. Students may wonder why it is there, and this can lead to some interesting discussions. Students may identify the teacher as a Christian because of the Bible, and they may ask questions about Christianity. One Christian teacher in the State of Washington reports that students have pointed to his Bible and said, "I didn't think you were allowed to have a Bible in a public school." You can imagine the interesting discussions that have ensued from comments like that!

Clearly, there are problems associated with the use of the Bible in the public school, but its use is far from prohibited. It is less than ideal when we are forced to treat the Bible as literature instead of as the inspired Word of God. But the author of Hebrews tells us that "the word of God is quick, and powerful, and sharper than any two-edged sword" (4:12). God's Word has power, and it can speak for itself and convict men's hearts, whenever and however it is presented.

The Creation-Evolution Controversy

Clarence Darrow, the defender of evolution in the Scopes trial, declared that, "It is bigotry for public schools to teach only one theory of origins." [14] And yet, in most public schools today only one theory of origins is taught—the theory of evolution. The exclusive and dogmatic teaching of evolution is, in the authors' views, not only an establishment of those religions which are compatible with evolution, but also a violation of the free exercise rights of those students and parents who believe in creation. And by keeping the creationist body of evidence from students, it restricts their right to know.

At present, it is unclear how far a teacher may go in teaching the creationist view of origins. In 1981 the State of Louisiana enacted a law which requires that, whenever origins are taught, creation must be given balanced treatment with evolution. The American Civil Liberties Union has challenged this law in the courts, and a federal district court granted summary judgment in favor of the ACLU. A three-judge circuit court of appeals panel unanimously affirmed the summary judgment, and then the entire circuit court, sitting *en banc*, affirmed the three-judge panel by a narrow vote of 8-7. The Supreme Court agreed to hear the case, and it was argued in December 1986. A ruling in *Edwards v. Aguillard* [15] is expected shortly. It could be a landmark ruling, or it might simply remand the case back to the lower courts for further proceedings. Those who are concerned about the creation/evolution controversy will need to watch this case closely to see what guidelines it ultimately provides.

At issue in the *Aguillard* case is whether the legislature may pass a law requiring that both sides be taught. The right of an individual teacher, on his own initiative, to teach the creationist view or the evolutionist view, or to give balanced treatment to both views is another matter. The ACLU takes the position that creationism is essentially a religious viewpoint and has no place in a science classroom. In several parts of the country the ACLU has threatened legal action against individual teachers for teaching creation, but with no definitive results to date. Many respected scientists take the position that the creation model and the evolution model are both scientific viewpoints. Even though both also have serious religious implications, both can be conceptualized in scientific terms, utilizing the scientific evidences and arguments for and against each.

If you are a creationist, you might well resent it if an evolutionist teacher were to indoctrinate your child with his viewpoint. It is important, therefore, to understand the concern a parent who believes in evolution would feel if his child is being indoctrinated with special creation. God has placed that child in the care and custody of his parent. Even if that parent is an unbeliever, a teacher has a duty to be sensitive to parental values. Rather than presenting only creation, both sides should be presented fairly—though that should not preclude a teacher from stating his own preference for one model or the other. And that is all creationists want. To our knowledge no creationist, anywhere, wants to ban evolution from the public schools. But many evolutionists want to ban creation!

How, then, should the controversy be handled? There are several possibilities. One is to present scientific evidences for both viewpoints, either from a text that presents both sides or by using more than one text. If this is to be presented as scientific evidence, it is perhaps best not to use the Bible or theological works.

This is entirely appropriate because the question of origins is, at least in part, a scientific question. The Christian teacher should not be cowed by the argument that creation cannot be scientific because it presupposes a Creator God. All forms of science have presuppositions, and there are many presuppositions inherent in the evolutionary model. For instance, it presupposes that spontaneous generation of life is possible, that an uncaused first cause exists, that an enormous amount of time exists for all this to be possible, and so forth. It could just as easily be argued that, instead of presupposing God, creation presents evidence for the existence of God. For example, if you are on a desert island, wondering if intelligent life had ever been there before, you might stumble upon a perfectly carved arrowhead in the sand. As you looked at that arrowhead, you would conclude that this was not merely a chance process of wind and erosion, but rather the work of an arrowhead maker. In just the same way, creation presents evidence for the existence of God.

But creation need not be limited to the science classroom. Regardless of how *Aguillard* is decided, one might consider the philosophical and theological ramifications of the creation/evolution controversy in the philosophy classroom, in a Bible as Literature class, in a comparative religion class, or in many others. In such a classroom one is not limited to scientific evidence. Rather, one might consider the Bible and other sources as well. The Christian teacher might point out the philosophical and theological problems associated with evolution. For example, what do we do with the many passages of the Bible which speak of special creation? How did the human soul or spirit come into being if we accept the evolutionary model? How did a non-physical soul or spirit evolve out of a physical animal? What is the source of human rights if we accept the evolutionary view? Do apes or ape-men have rights? Is the evolutionary view consistent with a belief in God-given absolute values? In assuming an upward direction of history from the slime to the stars, is the evolutionary view of history consistent with reality? These are weighty matters for discussion, and they are not off-limits in the public schools.

Let us suppose the courts decide to ban all mention of creation in the public schools. The Christian who teaches science might still present the scientific evidence for and against evolution. The teacher might point out the glaring gaps in the fossil record, the lack of transitory fossils between fixed species. He might also point out the evidence for a young universe. For example, the recent Voyager satellite discovered volcanic activity on one of Jupiter's moons indicating a hot, liquid center which would have cooled and hardened long ago given its distance from the sun, if the solar system were billions of years old as evolutionists believe. But what does the teacher do when a student asks, "Well, if evolution is false, what's the alternative?" That's not clear. A teacher might have to say, "Because of school policy and court rulings, I'm not allowed to answer that. If you want an answer, I suggest you talk to your pastor."

There are other possibilities. An outside speaker, a scientist, a pastor, or other informed creationist can be invited to present the creationist view to your class. Students might be given an option to read a creationist book instead of the normal evolutionary textbook. You might ask the school librarian to purchase some creationist books for the school library. If you do, be ready to suggest several good ones. (See the chapter on Sources of Help.) Or, you might purchase some creationist books for the library yourself, or get your church to help you.

The evolutionary dogmatists have tried diligently to create a monopoly in our classrooms, but they do not have a stranglehold yet. Within these limits, the creationist view may still be presented.

Values Clarification

Values clarification courses in the public school have been a source of controversy in recent years. On the one hand, Christians generally want values to be taught in the public schools. The concept of "value-free" education is totally unworkable for, if successful, it will produce a generation of educated monsters whose heads are filled with technical information but who have no moral values with which to use their knowledge for good instead of evil.

But values clarification programs, as they are currently taught, are a cause of legitimate concern. All too often they represent humanistic ways of making value judgments, relying solely upon reason, experience, or utilitarianism. Forming values based upon the pronouncements of God's revealed Word, or the lessons of persons in authority such as parents or pastors, is strongly discouraged.

Values clarification programs commonly present problem situations that are designed to lead students to think in terms of relative, situational ethics. One such problem situation involves a life raft containing a certain number of persons including a football star, a pregnant woman, a doctor, a pastor, etc. There is only enough food for a certain number of people. So to save the rest, some of the people must be thrown overboard. The question to be resolved is: Whom would you choose to live and who would die? Many Christians object that this encourages the student to "play God" and that it implies that some human lives are worth more than others. Another problem involves the question of whether to steal food for your starving grandmother, implying that the commandment, "Thou shalt not steal," is somehow less than absolute.

Despite the objectionable features of values clarification programs, they do open the door for the presentation of Christian values if handled properly. Even using the values clarification materials currently available for public schools, the Christian teacher can neutralize the objectionable features and present positive Christian values instead. In discussing the means of formulating values, the Christian teacher could go beyond the text. He could explain that many people believe man is incapable of learning ultimate truth through his own reason and intelligence, but that God has revealed His truths and His values through His Word, the Bible, and that God has placed parents, pastors, and teachers in positions of authority over children so that children may learn from their teaching and example.

While discussing some of the various problems presented in values clarification materials, the teacher should feel free to question the texts and go beyond them. In dealing with the lifeboat example, he might point out the dangers of letting one person decide who should live and who should die, and suggest that another alternative exists: Praying, leaving the matter in the hands of God, and deciding that all human lives are equally precious so either all will live or die together. A values clarification course can also be an excellent opportunity to make use of alternative materials or guest speakers.

Sex Education

Like values clarification, sex education is a field of controversy. Parents generally want their children to learn about sex, but many question whether the schools are promoting sex education at much too early an age. Many Christian parents and educators believe that sex education at too early an age is not only unnecessary but can lead to an unhealthy interest in sex. Many believe the proper place to teach sex education is the home or the church.

Furthermore, sex is a value-laden subject. Many parents believe it is dangerous to teach children the "raw facts" about sex without teaching moral values as well. But if the schools teach moral values about sex, whose values will they teach? Christian parents complain that such programs fail to teach the Judeo-Christian view of sex. All too often, sex education courses refuse to teach that sexual intercourse outside of marriage is wrong. Often they teach children that their sexual practices are their own business and that neither parents nor pastors nor anyone else may tell them what to do. Sometimes they teach children that premarital and extramarital sex are all right so long as people really care about each other and act responsibly to prevent disease and unwanted pregnancy. Sometimes they teach that sodomy, homosexuality, lesbianism, and even beastiality and incest are acceptable lifestyles. Some such programs teach abortion as a legitimate means of birth control, but do not mention abstinence as an alternative.

As this is being written, the nation is threatened with an AIDS epidemic. Many national leaders in education, liberal and conservative alike, advocate massive programs of AIDS education in our schools, including instruction in how to obtain and use condoms. Christians are in a dilemma over programs like these. Certainly Christians want the nation's children to be informed about the danger of AIDS. But partially out of fear of offending homosexuals as a minority group, the programs currently being promoted downplay the fact that AIDS is transmitted primarily through sexual activity, and particularly homosexual activity. These programs also tend to ignore the fact that condoms are not a reliable means of preventing AIDS disease. Because of these objections, Christians are often labeled as opposing AIDS education and sex education entirely.

How should a Christian teacher handle sex education? By using the right of academic freedom, coupled with the constitutional right of students to know the *whole* truth, to give the full facts on matters like these. The Christian teacher has every right, after fully covering the subject matter, to state a personal preference for abstinence from sex outside of marriage, and to present the case for abstinence. For example, the teacher is free to explain the dangers of sexual promiscuity to the individual and to society: the fact that sexual involvement frequently leads to emotional involvement and ultimate trauma, the fact of unwanted pregnancies, the fact of guilt feelings later on, the fact of disease. The teacher should feel free to mention the study by Dr. J.D. Unwin who, after examining eighty primitive cultures and sixteen modern cultures, concluded that no society can maintain a high level of civilization over an extended period of time, unless sexual energy is contained through monogamous marriage. [16]

In discussing alternate lifestyles, the teacher should feel free

73

to discuss the problems of a homosexual lifestyle: The guilt, the high crime rate, the high suicide rate, and others. [17] And when the subject of abortion is considered, the teacher should feel free to present the extensive medical evidence which demonstrates that the unborn child is a living human being from the point of conception, the alternatives to abortion, and the longterm emotional trauma abortion causes for the mother who chooses that alternative. [18]

After having covered these matters, academic freedom entitles the teacher to explain, in a non-indoctrinating way, the Judeo-Christian view of sex as taught in the Bible.

In the above paragraphs we have expressed our view of academic freedom as applied to this subject. Since the Supreme Court has not ruled definitively on the matter, we cannot guarantee that the teacher who follows this course of action will never face a problem with his superiors. It is our opinion, however, that if the matter goes to court, the teacher who follows this course of action will ultimately prevail.

Music

Recently, at a church conference, a public school music teacher asked for advice. His principal objected to his practice of using religious songs in his choral music. He wondered if he was within his rights to do so.

The Eighth Circuit Court of Appeals ruled in 1981 that a school Christmas program may include religious carols so long as they are presented "in a prudent and objective manner and as a traditional part of the cultural and religious heritage of the particular holiday." [19] This is the position most courts are likely to take. Since religious music is part of our cultural heritage, and since familiarizing students with our cultural heritage is a legitimate secular purpose of education, religious music may be used in public school music programs if it is presented in a balanced way. If the music teacher used entirely religious music, that might be objectionable; but if the religious music is balanced with other kinds of music, he is probably within his rights.

Much of our nation's patriotic music contains references to God. Songs like "God Bless America" and "God of Our Fathers" contain obvious religious overtones. "America the Beautiful" includes the repeated line, "America, America, God shed His grace on thee," and the fourth stanza of "My Country 'Tis of Thee" begins, "Our fathers' God, to Thee, Author of liberty, to Thee we sing." Even our national anthem contains the lines in the fourth stanza, "Then conquer we must, When our cause it is just, And this be our motto, In God is our trust." Since inculcation of patriotism is obviously a legitimate secular purpose of education, these songs certainly may be used in public school programs.

Religious Holidays

How would you feel if you were told that a colossal birthday party, the event of the year, was to be held in your honor? But there were three restrictions: (1) You may not attend; (2) Your name may not be mentioned; and (3) Your picture may not be displayed. That's exactly how some of the radical separationists would have us celebrate the birthday of Jesus Christ.

Fortunately, the courts have not gone that far—yet. As we have seen, religious Christmas carols are permissible if presented in good taste, with balance, and as part of our cultural heritage. The display of manger scenes on public property has been upheld [20] and would probably be permissible in a school setting as well.

One might point out that many pagan rites are associated with the so-called secular versions of Christmas. Holly and mistletoe were ancient pagan symbols, yet the radical separationists do not object to their use at Christmas. While the separationists object to crosses and empty tombs at Easter, they do not object to Easter bunnies and Easter eggs even though these were pagan fertility symbols. They object to songs of thankfulness at Thanksgiving, but not to black cats and witches at Halloween even though these are occult symbols. Paganism is a religion, too. If the establishment of Christianity is wrong, so is the establishment of paganism. [21]

This might be a good place to impart some words of wisdom from Norman Lamb, a prominent Oklahoma state senator. "If you ask the same question enough times, eventually you're bound to get a wrong answer." While it is wise to discreetly check out school policies before taking action, sometimes it is better to simply assume you have the right to express your faith rather than asking specifically. Questions like, "May I put up a manger scene in my room?" "May I place a figure of the Christ child on our class Christmas tree?" "May we include 'Silent Night' in the Christmas program?" invite a "no" answer. In a "gray" area, if you assume you are within your rights, most likely others will make the same assumption. If you are challenged, then you can decide whether to assert your rights or to plead ignorance and back down.

Religious holiday observations usually can be included if presented discreetly, in good taste, and in a way that can be clearly related to legitimate educational objectives. Ask your students, "Why do we celebrate Christmas?" "Why was the birth of Christ a significant event in world history?" "What is the meaning of Easter?" "Why was Christ's resurrection considered important by Christians?" "Why would anyone call the day of Christ's crucifixion 'Good' Friday?" "Why is November 1 called 'All Saints' Day'?" "What is a 'saint,' anyway?" By asking such questions of your students and gently pointing them to the answers, you not only educate them as to their cultural heritage, you point them to Jesus Christ as well.

Student Participation

As we have seen, the teacher is free to express an opinion, but is not free to indoctrinate his students in a narrow and dogmatic manner. However, you can encourage student participation by asking questions.

Most likely, shortly after the school year begins, you will have some idea which students hold Christian values and which students express Christian values well. You can obtain their help by directing questions to them. "John, how does your family celebrate Christmas?" "Mary, what do you think Jefferson meant when he wrote 'the laws of nature and of nature's God'?" "Darrell, do you agree with Darwin's theory of survival of the fittest?" Peer pressure means a great deal to students of all ages. Your ideas are more likely to be seen as credible if the class sees that other students support them.

Also, you should encourage your Christian students to question you. You have more freedom to speak on Christian subjects in response to student questions than on your own initiative.

In addition to class discussion, you can encourage your students to do outside research and present it to the class. Suppose Bill timidly ventures during history class, "I heard somewhere, maybe it was Sunday School, that when the settlers landed at Jamestown they set up a cross." You could respond, "That's fascinating, Bill. Could you please try to remember where you learned that, or check it out in the library, and give us a report about it? You'll get extra credit!"

When assigning book reports or term papers, encourage Christian students to choose Christian books or Christian topics. Then it's a good idea to have them share what they have learned with the rest of the class. In so doing, you have not only witnessed to the class, but you have also taught your Christian students to be more effective witnesses as well.

Outside Speakers

The outside speaker probably has more freedom to express himself than the teacher has because he is less likely to be perceived as an agent of the state. Furthermore, if he oversteps his bounds, there is little school officials can do about it except not invite him back.

On controversial topics, the teacher may find that outside speakers are eager to share their views at no cost, and they may be better informed than the teacher on a specific topic. Too, the teacher can avoid being directly identified with a controversial issue if an outside speaker presents the case instead.

The Christian teacher might look to such groups as the local affiliate of Right to Life, Eagle Forum, or Concerned Women for America for capable spokespersons on such issues as creation/ evolution, abortion, school prayer, and many others. Someone from the Veterans of Foreign Wars or the American Legion might be willing to discuss patriotism or defense policies.

Outside speakers can provide refreshing points of view and are sometimes a welcome change from the daily routine of the classroom. Do not be afraid to occasionally invite an outside speaker whose view differs from your own. Truthful objectivity requires a balanced presentation.

Parental Involvement

As stated before, the authors believe God has placed children in the care and custody of their parents, and that parental wishes in education should be afforded great respect. When parents object to a particular text, outside reading, or other matters on religious or other grounds, their objections should be accommodated whenever possible. This doesn't mean the child should be allowed to get out of an assignment. Rather, he should be required to complete another assignment that is equally difficult and challenging. The parent's help can be solicited in choosing and supervising such an assignment: "I respect your views even if I don't agree with them, Mrs. Anderson. If possible, I will allow your child to do a different project instead. May I ask you and your husband to come up with an alternative project and call me back?" You should take this position even if the parent's views are very different from yours. In God's economy, a Moslem, a Buddhist, an atheist, or even a Communist parent has as much right to the care and custody of his child as does a Christian.

Parents can also be a tremendous resource for the teacher.

Each parent has certain special interests and talents that can be utilized in your teaching. Some may be pastors, doctors, lawyers. Some may have special interests in woodworking, the outdoors, literature, or classical music that can enrich the entire class. Do not hesitate to call upon parents for help.

This is especially true of Christian parents. You might call upon them for presentation of Christian themes. This must, of course, be done with tact, discretion, and balance, but parental support can be a great asset. You might also confer occasionally with Christian parents about your special desire to share Christ with your students and ask their suggestions as to how to proceed.

Literature

We have already seen that the Bible may be used in public school classrooms, subject to certain limitations. In addition, there is much literature that presents Christian themes.

For example, C.S. Lewis's *The Chronicles of Narnia* is filled with Christian symbols, themes, values, and archetypes, but *The Chronicles* are read and loved by many non-Christians because nowhere is Jesus Christ expressly mentioned. The same is true of Lewis's space trilogy. *The Chronicles* could be used anywhere from grade school to adult level; the others should probably be limited to junior high school and above. For grade school students, one might read the Sugar Creek Gang series, or the various books of Matilda Nordtvedt, Lee Roddy, Jerry Jenkins, or Hilda Stahl. Laura Ingalls Wilder's *Little House on the Prairie* series, while not expressly Christian, certainly draws upon Christian values.

Also, much, if not most, classical literature draws upon the Bible and/or expresses Judeo-Christian values. There is no way all of this can be completely excised from our cultural heritage.

Religious Symbols

In the *Tinker* case previously cited, the Supreme Court upheld the right of students to wear black armbands to protest the war in Vietnam. Likewise, the Second Circuit Court of Appeals has noted that "There is little room . . . in the majestic generalities of the Bill of Rights . . . for an interpretation of the First Amendment that would be more restrictive with respect to teachers than it is with respect to their students, where there has been no interference with the requirements of appropriate discipline in the operation of the school." [22] Since teachers have essentially the same First Amendment rights as students, and since freedom of expression may not be curtailed just because it touches upon a religious subject, the right of the Christian teacher to wear religious symbols seems to be constitutionally protected.

Once again, the teacher must bear in mind the crucial, but extremely fine, distinction between his role as citizen with constitutional rights and his role as an agent of the State. What he wears on his person will almost always be considered a matter of individual expression rather than state action. There is some case precedent for the premise that wearing full clerical garb in a public school classroom may be prohibited, but anything short of that seems to be a constitutional right.

What about religious symbols or other religious materials on one's desk? Once again, that which is on the teacher's desk would appear to be personal rather than state related. A Bible on one's desk is an effective and permissible witness. Other religious symbols or religious materials would probably be permissible if they are displayed and used in good taste.

The more removed from the teacher's person the religious material is, though, the more likely it is to be perceived as state sponsored. The bulletin board is more removed from the teacher's person than the desk. While the teacher has some freedom to express his personality and his views on the bulletin board, anything on it is more likely to be perceived as state sponsored. Religious materials on the bulletin board are not totally forbidden, but must be balanced and must relate to some legitimate educational purpose.

After Hours

What a teacher says and does is less likely to be perceived as state action when done outside of class. Informal discussions on religious subjects between classes are more likely to be permissible than during class. Such discussions before and after school hours are more likely to be upheld than between classes. Such discussions off the school premises are even more likely to be upheld.

In one sense a teacher, like a military person, is "on duty" twenty-four hours a day. Even off-campus his words and actions reflect to some extent upon the school. But he has great freedom to interact with his students during off-hours provided there is no school policy to the contrary. Normally this would include the right to invite students to his home.

While this opens great opportunities, it should be done with great caution. The teacher who socializes with his students may be perceived as having an immoral purpose in mind. (Needless to say, this danger is greater with students of the opposite sex.) Such socialization should be with groups of students, almost never one-on-one.

And some parents might feel threatened by such socialization. He may feel the teacher is taking his (the parent's) rightful place in the child's life. And, if the parent is not a Christian, he may feel the teacher is undermining his right to form his child's religious values, just as you would feel if a non-Christian teacher were spending time with your child. Such socialization should therefore involve the parent as well as the student as much as possible, and should always include the parent's written permission.

Special Note:

On June 19, 1987, just as this book was going to press, the Supreme Court ruled in *Aguillard v. Edwards* that Louisiana's law requiring balanced treatment of creation and evolution was unconstitutional because the legislative purpose was clearly religious rather than secular. The decision does not prohibit teachers from presenting the creationist viewpoint. In fact, the Court said that "teaching a variety of scientific theories about the origin of humankind to schoolchildren might be validly done with the clear secular intent of enhancing the effectiveness of science instruction." The Court said further, "we do not imply that a legislature could never require that scientific critiques of prevailing scientific theories be taught." Unless, and until, the Court says otherwise, teachers and school boards should feel free to present the creationist position, provided they do so in a non-dogmatic manner. In addition, legislatures might consider a bill which would require science teachers to present the evidence for and against evolution.

FOOTNOTES

[1] Ann Wharton, "Teachers and Their Civil Rights," *Fundamentalist Journal*, December 1986, pp. 60-62.

[2] *Engel v. Vitale*, 370 U.S. 421 (1962).

[3] Bonnie Bergren, "A Christian Teacher in a Public School," *Light and Life*, April 1987, pp. 14-15.

[4] *Vincent v. Widmar*, 454 U.S. 263 (1981).

[5] *Bender v. Williamsport Area School District*, 89 L.Ed.2d. 501, 475 U.S._____, 106 S. Ct. _____ (March 25, 1986).

[6] *McCollum v. Board of Education*, 333 U.S. 203 (1948).

[7] *Zorach v. Clauson*, 343 U.S. 306 (1952).

[8] *Abington Township v. Schempp*, 374 U.S. 203 (1963).

[9] Horace Mann, Letter, 1944, quoted by Lynn Buzzard, *Schools: They Haven't Got a Prayer* (Elgin, Illinois: David C. Cook, 1982), p. 99.

[10] Horace Mann, quoted by Leo Pfeffer, *Church, State and Freedom* rev. ed. (Boston: Beacon Press, 1967), p. 285; quoted by Buzzard, p. 99.

[11] James Applegate, et. al., eds., *Adventures in World Literature* (New York: Harcourt Brace Jovanovich, 1970), p. 23.

[12] Joyce Vedral, "I Teach Bible in a Public School," *Christian Herald*, September 1982 pp. 18,12,16; quoted by Buzzard, pp. 165-168.

[13] My thanks to Lynn Buzzard and his book *Schools: They Haven't Got a Prayer* for bringing these sources to my attention.

[14] Clarence Darrow, quoted by R. O'Bannon, "Creation, Evolution, and Public Education," #5 Dayton Symposium on Tennessee's Evolution Laws, May 18, 1974; quoted by Wendell R. Bird, "Freedom of Religion and Science Instruction in Public Schools," *Yale Law Journal*, Vol. 87, No. 3 (January 1978), p. 561.

[15] *Edwards v. Aguillard*, 765 F.2d 1251 (5th Cir. 1985); Rehearing en banc. 778 F.2d 225 (5th Cir. 1985); _____ U.S. _____ (1987).

[16] J.D. Unwin, *Sex and Culture* (Oxford: Oxford University Press, 1934, pp. viii, 23, 340, 414, 431, 618, 618; cited by O.R. Johnston, *Who Needs the Family?* (Downers Grove, Illinois: InterVarsity Press, 1979), pp. 43-44.

[17] See generally, Tim LaHaye, *What Everyone Should Know About Homosexuality* (Wheaton, Illinois: Tyndale, 1980).

[18] See generally, *Christian Action Council Resource Manual*, available through Christian Action Council.

[19] *Florey v. Sioux Falls School District*, 619 F.2d 1311 (8th Cir. 1980).

[20] *Lynch v. Donnelly*, 465 U.S. 688 (1984).

[21] *Man, Myth and Magic: An Illustrated Encyclopedia of the Supernatural* (New York: Marshall Cavendish Corporation, 1970); See Cat 3:417; Egg 6:781; Hares 9:1210; Holly 10:1329; Mistletoe 14:1860; Witch 22:3041.

[22] *Russo v. Central School District No. 1, Town of Rush v. County of Monroe, State of New York*, 469 F.2d 623 (2nd Cir., 1972), cert. den. 411 U.S. 923 (1973).

Chapter 5

Meeting Pupils' Instructional Needs: Establishing Accountability

As we have seen in the preceding chapters, the teacher has several personal rights guaranteed under the law, the Constitution, and the state and federal statutes regulating education. But what about the teacher's responsibilities to the State? While these legal protections apply to all teachers, the Christian teacher recognizes a higher responsibility.

Whatever you do, do your work heartily, as for the Lord rather than for men. Colossians 3:23 (NASB)

Let all who are under the yoke as slaves regard their own masters as worthy of all honor so that the name of God and our doctrine may not be spoken against. I Timothy 6:1 (NASB)

So how do the legal responsibilities of education affect the Christian teacher in a public school? In the next several chapters we will discuss various critical areas of education and responsibility.

A front page story in *The Denver Post* in January of 1987 grabbed the attention of concerned educators throughout the State of Colorado. Similar stories across the country prior to the Denver case had brought into increasing focus a problem faced by educators—with varying levels of success—for years. Simply stated, the problem had to do with grouping children for instruction to individualize teaching. Denver, like other school districts across the country, had gotten into trouble quite by accident. The newspaper account was to-the-point.

The Denver Public Schools should re-evaluate 3,000 black and Hispanic students to determine if they were improperly assigned to the district's programs for the mentally retarded, emotionally disturbed, learning disabled and speech defective, experts say.

In a report to be released today, a team of outside auditors said the Denver schools rely excessively on biased IQ tests to place students in special education programs.

As a result, minorities are "significantly over-represented" in the programs, and some students have been mislabeled and assigned to classes where they may not get the help they need, said the experts. [1]

In other districts, courts and educators had condemned various measures of ability as culturally biased, discriminatory, and generally inaccurate. Stories of normal children being misassigned to classes for the developmentally disabled surfaced with regularity. Knowledgeable teachers, principals, and other school professionals were naturally concerned about their liability to lawsuits resulting from mis-placing or mis-grouping pupils for instruction. The problem was not one which could be ignored. Teachers were in a difficult position. Since a typical class of 25 pupils represents a tremendous span of achievement levels, teachers could be charged legitimately with incompetence if they did not attempt to individualize instruction. On the other hand, teachers knew that they could not possibly individualize instruction for every child in every subject. The sheer logistics of such a task—addressing learning levels, rates, styles, interests, conducting assessment, record-keeping, supervision, and actual teaching itself—presented an impossible demand. The alternative seemed, to many teachers, to be that of grouping children into instructional groups. But even then, many teachers felt anxious because of cases similar to the Denver Public Schools case. It was the classic case of being totally open to criticism and totally vulnerable to professional problems, regardless of what they did. However, although the problem of grouping and individualizing is a *difficult* one to solve, and although the potential for professional liability is *significant*, it is not impossible to solve. The potential for professional liability can be *significantly reduced*.

Can You Stay Out of Trouble? A "Grouping Exercise"

A large group has been described in the situation presented below. The large group can be subdivided into smaller groups in which the members have certain characteristics in common. (An example of a subgroup formed from the large group described below might be "males-females.")

Divide the large group into as many subgroups as possible. List the subgroups in the *most logical order* in the box below.

On a certain ranch in eastern Colorado there is a large herd of cattle. Some of the cattle are males and some are females. Among the males, there are both steers and bulls. Among the females, some cattle can be found which do not give milk. A part of the herd is comprised of calves. The cattle in the herd are either black or brown. All of the cattle with horns are brown, but not all of the brown cattle have horns. A part of the herd is made up of dairy cattle; the other part of the herd is made up of beef cattle. The cattle in the herd are from Texas, Wyoming, and Colorado. Some of the cattle are fed hay, and some of the cattle are on green grass. Not all of the cattle from Colorado have eaten green grass.

The rancher has asked you, a beginning cowboy, to divide the herd into as many subgroups as possible (on paper) according to what you consider to be the most logical or most important order. The rancher will base his decision regarding your possible permanent employment on how well you do the job. (Assume that you need the job.)

Allow yourself five minutes to work on the problem above. Then check your answer on the following pages. [2]

Important Factors to Consider

Let's take a look at some important factors that should be considered in the preceding exercise.

First, regardless of how you grouped the cattle, you cannot be sure that you grouped them in the most logical order since you did not know the rancher's purpose for grouping the cattle. In order to defend your grouping decisions, you have to know the purpose for grouping.

If the rancher's primary purpose was to have his cattle grouped on the criterion of whether or not they had horns, you would not form your final groups on the basis of their color because this criterion would be totally unrelated to the rancher's purpose.

If, on the other hand, the rancher's primary purpose was to group all of his black cattle to ship to market, you would first group the cattle on the basis of their color. This would group them according to the rancher's primary purpose.

Similarly, unless a teacher has a specific purpose in mind when he groups children for instruction, it would be very difficult to defend a specific grouping plan. For example, a teacher might group children into "fast," "average," and "special attention" groups for a class in reading instruction. The teacher might use a defensible criterion for grouping, such as the

Instructional Reading Level of each child. But, if the teacher uses the same Instructional Reading Level criteria of "fast," "average," and "special attention"—comprised of the same children—for a class in math, the teacher's method of grouping would be open to criticism. The teacher would be legally vulnerable. Reading skill levels cannot be used to determine grouping in non-reading classes.

There are several significant facts for teachers to bear in mind if they decide to group children for instruction.

First, any group in which the members of the group have been selected on the basis of some common characteristic or characteristics is called a homogeneous group. Since most groups are similar only in reference to a limited number of common characteristics, it should be kept in mind that, when grouping children for instruction, the groups would be similar only in reference to a limited number of common characteristics.

The first principle of effective grouping is that a purpose for grouping must be established before grouping can take place. It is absolutely defensible for a teacher to attempt to make groups homogeneous by focusing on characteristics related to a specific instructional purpose.

Some common characteristics, or criteria, which have been used to group children for reading instruction are:

reading achievement scores	social maturity
readiness	interest
physical maturity	intelligence
mental age	friendship preferences
chronological age	personality traits
reading skills	language facility

Even though homogeneous groups could be established on the basis of one or more of these common characteristics, the groups could be heterogenous on the basis of the remaining characteristics.

Since there are so many characteristics which can be used to group children for instruction, it is advisable that the selection of a characteristic or characteristics should always be conducted in relation to a specific instructional purpose. Other defensible reasons for grouping children into specific groups would be the nature of the child, the nature of the material, or the nature of the specific instructional activity.

It is impossible to avoid criticism in responding to the challenge of individual differences among children in a classroom. Regardless of which criterion or which combinations of criteria for grouping are used, it is virtually impossible to establish groups which are homogeneous in all respects. Each criterion for grouping, when examined in relation to a specific purpose, could possess certain advantages and certain disadvantages. What is of paramount importance in protecting yourself against charges of incompetence or against legal liability is to be able to provide defensible reasons for *why* you do or do not group children into certain groups, and to be able to defend the criterion or criteria you used in the process of grouping them.

Avoid Grouping Problems by Individualizing Instruction

One rule of thumb in anticipating differences among children is this: "The minimal expected range of achievement in any given classroom is equal to the number on the classroom door." Obviously, if you're in room 32 or some other room where the number doesn't show grade level, the rule of thumb doesn't apply! But if you are a sixth grade teacher, and if there is a "6" on your door, you can expect that there will be a six-year span of achievement between the highest and the lowest pupils in your classroom. If it's grade three you teach, then you can expect at least a three-year difference, and so on. The fact that a wide range of achievement is a "given" suggests that a competent teacher must attempt to individualize instruction.

But when one considers the fact that children are different in the ways they learn, in the rates at which they learn, in their interests, in their abilities, in their aptitudes, in their ability to work independently, and in a multitude of other traits, the usual reaction to individualizing instruction is one of panic. Few teachers believe that they can initiate and sustain an "individualized" program, principally because their concept of individualized instruction is that of one-to-one teaching. This idea is erroneous; it has probably defeated more teachers who made a conscientious effort to provide for individual differences than it has helped because the task of providing one-to-one teaching is so monumental and impractical that most teachers cannot or will not attempt it.

There are two steps toward successfully meeting the challenge of the wide range of achievement which exists in your classroom. The first step is to recognize that there are *degrees* of individualization of instruction. It does not require one-to-one teaching. The second step is to accept the idea that you can find a degree of individualization which fits you, your students, and your unique teaching situation, and which can be defended.

Three classroom variables can be manipulated by you to achieve varying degrees of individualization of instruction. For purposes of discussion, these variables are called "teacher input," "materials," and "student output." A brief description of each variable follows:

Teacher input: Any method used by a teacher to convey information, develop ideas, or encourage thinking prior to assigning independent study. Teacher input includes lectures, demonstrations, discussion, and the use of audio-visual materials or equipment.

Materials: Any source to which the student can turn in order to expand upon the information, idea, or concept introduced through the teacher's input. The student might independently listen to a tape, watch a film, read a chapter, conduct research, or utilize any other resources which might be available.

Student Output: Any project, assignment or other activity which is required by the teacher as practice or as evidence of a student's understanding of the information, idea, or concept developed through teacher input and materials used.

When no manipulation of variables takes place, no individualization of instruction takes place. For example, consider a classroom in which there are thirty students. There is no attempt to adjust teacher input to groups of students. The teacher provides one presentation in the form of a filmstrip which introduces a concept in science. Each student has the same basic text for the class, and all students read the same chapter. There is no attempt to match students with appropriate materials. After reading the material, all students reproduce a diagram and answer three questions prepared by the teacher. There is no attempt to provide assignments which match students' abilities or interests. Furthermore, the teacher expects the same level of achievement from each student.

Now consider a classroom where a degree of individualization is taking place. The teacher provides only one presentation in the form of a filmstrip which introduces a concept in science. Each student reads the same chapter. After reading the chapter, however, some students are assigned the drawing of a diagram and the completing of questions prepared by the teacher. Other students are directed to additional reading. Still other students are required to view some slides. The only variable was that of student output; nevertheless, some individualization of instruction took place.

Another classroom might manipulate two variables. In this classroom, the teacher, like the other teachers, provides one presentation in the form of a filmstrip. The teacher then asks students to read about the presentation in one of several books which are available. Students are provided with one of several assignments. In this classroom, an even greater degree of individualization has taken place.

Manipulation of variables and the corresponding degree of individualization are shown in the accompanying diagram. The right hand side of the diagram shows no manipulation of variables, and, hence, no individualization of instruction. The left hand side of the chart shows manipulation of all three variables, and, hence, a great degree of individualization of instruction. The middle parts of the chart show manipulation of one or more variables and the corresponding degree of individualization of instruction which can be accomplished.

A look at the diagram reveals that when a teacher spends no time and expends no effort in attempting to individualize instruction (top arrow, right side) students will probably have to spend much time and expend much effort and attain only very limited results (bottom arrow, right side). What is economical for the teacher is not economical for the student. Conversely, as the teacher spends more time and effort in attempting to individualize instruction (top arrow, left side), the student will probably need to spend less time and expend less effort in attaining greater gains (bottom arrow, left side) than he achieved when his time and effort were not properly directed. When this occurs, what is increasingly less economical for the teacher is increasingly more economical for the student. Simply stated, the less time and effort a teacher puts into manipulating variables to meet individual differences, the more time and effort a student will have to put in, and the student's time and effort will probably be unproductive. The more time and effort a teacher puts into manipulating variables, the less time and effort a student will have to put in, and the student's time and effort will probably be more productive.

The main idea illustrated by the diagram is this: *Individualization of instruction occurs in varying degrees.* Somewhere along the continuum shown in the diagram there should be a plan which fits you and your teaching situation. You should tackle

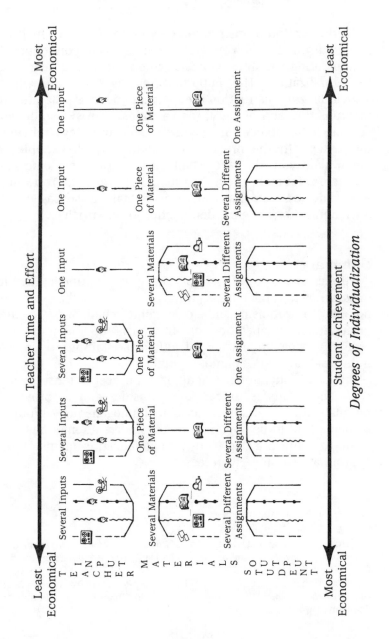

individualization of instruction only on the level at which you are comfortable. As you gain expertise and confidence in manipulating variables, you can attain increasing degrees of individualization. The important fact is that you will be individualizing instruction the moment you take a step toward manipulating one of the three variables. You will be demonstrating competence in the area of addressing individual differences. In the process of deciding which variables to manipulate, you will have established careful consideration of the *reasons* for making your instructional decisions. You will be able to demonstrate that your decision making was based upon a thoughtful and logical deliberation of alternatives.

Summary

Public and private schools have come under fire for misdiagnosing and misassigning students. Teachers are vulnerable to criticism and to credible challenges to their professional competence on the basis of inappropriately grouping their pupils, or of otherwise failing to address individual differences among pupils.

From an educational standpoint, the best defense against such allegations is to carefully consider and to provide a rationale for the criterion used in homogeneously grouping students, and to demonstrate that a sincere attempt has been made to achieve a degree of individualization of instruction appropriate for any given lesson.

FOOTNOTES

[1] *The Denver Post*, January 22, 1987, p. 1A.

[2] Burron, Arnold H., and Claybaugh, Amos L., *Basic Concepts in Reading Instruction: A Programmed Approach*, Columbus, Ohio: Charles E. Merrill Publishing Company, 1977. (Second Edition), p. 79.

[3] Burron, Arnold H., and Claybaugh, Amos L., *Using Reading to Teach Subject Matter: Fundamentals for Content Teachers*, Columbus, Ohio: Charles E. Merrill Publishing Company, 1974, p. 72.

Chapter 6

Making Sound Instructional Decisions: Nine Key Steps

In late 1986, expectant parents in Cheyenne, Wyoming were dismayed to discover that no obstetricians were available for medical care. Liability insurance costs, fueled by unbridled lawsuits, had driven every obstetrician out of the city.

The advent and increasing viability of the "Parents' Rights" movement in the United States, with resultant pressure on professional educators from all sides, has fostered a climate paralleling that of the medical profession. Increasingly, textbook publishers have felt pressure, by sheer economic necessity in some instances and by duly constituted authority in other instances, to change the content of their materials. School districts and school personnel have felt the heat of local parental challenges to the appropriateness of methods, materials, or content in public school classrooms, and they have reacted to the implications of state and national court decisions on their deliberations concerning these elements.

Item: In Tennessee, the court upheld the right of parents to make available for their children alternative materials to replace materials to which they objected.

Item: In California, textbooks which included a creationist perspective were rejected by an evolution-oriented board of education.

Item: In Alabama, a federal district court upheld the contention of Christian parents and teachers that a substantial number of textbooks unconstitutionally promoted the religion of secular humanism.

Item: In Georgia, a teacher with over twenty years of experience was dismissed for showing "Blue Thunder," an R-rated movie, to his middle school pupils. He had not previewed the movie; he had incorrectly concluded that it was as benign as a television series of the same name. His inability to adequately defend his decision cost him his job.

Item: People for the American Way, Norman Lear's liberal organization, produced a skillfully prepared electronic polemic castigating the far right for alleged attempts to stifle the freedom to learn. Their videotape, narrated by an earnest and imploring Burt Lancaster, was shown to captive audiences of public school teachers during mandatory in-service eduation sessions.

Item: On April 10, 1987, the *Rocky Mountain News* [1] carried a story about a high school business teacher who was formally protesting an order by school administrators to remove bulletin board posters of quotations from Abraham Lincoln, Thomas Jefferson, George Washington, and Squanto, the Indian friend of the Pilgrims. The quotations contained references to God, and even though the school superintendent commended the teacher's efforts to "spread the Good News," he added that, "the basic point of these posters is not patriotism but promotion of the Christian faith," and that the teacher's classroom was not the proper forum for such activity. The teacher has taught for nine years in Steamboat Springs, Colorado, the district which is protesting her use of the posters. She has argued that the order from the superintendent violates her academic freedom. But what is of primary interest in this case can best be illustrated by citing the position of both the superintendent and the teacher, as reported in the *Rocky Mountain News*.

The superintendent "maintains academic freedom is not at issue, particularly because the posters have nothing to do with the subject matter that Davis teaches" *(emphasis added).*

"Davis concedes the materials have little to do with her business class *(emphasis added). But she adds that other teachers in the district use bulletin board materials that do not*

bear directly on class subjects."

At this writing, school officials and the Steamboat Springs School District's attorney are reviewing a letter from the teacher's attorney, and the district is reviewing its policy on bulletin board materials. It seems clear, though, that had the teacher specifically identified a good reason for including the posters on her bulletin board, she could have precluded any continuing controversy about her decision.

Undeniably, in each of the situations described above and in similar situations reported repeatedly across the country, one conclusion is inescapable: Teachers will be increasingly called upon to justify their decisions. They will have to have a good reason for including or excluding specific information or points-of-view on potentially controversial issues. They will have to have a good reason for identifying specific course objectives, to the exclusion of other, equally desirable objectives. They will have to have a good reason for selecting any potentially controversial instructional vehicle (book, film, videotape, etc.) to the exclusion of any other equally desirable and readily available instructional vehicle. The public will press teachers—in the courts if necessary—for objectivity, for sensitivity to the values and beliefs of the clients of the schools, and for psychologically and pedagogically defensible instructional decisions. The authors are convinced that recent decisions of the courts which have been favorable to both liberals *and* traditionalists will serve to stimulate, rather than to quell, emerging parent activism. Therefore, to protect their rights, teachers need to be able to defend all of their decisions related to *what* is taught (content), *how* it is taught (method), or *by what vehicle* it is taught (materials).

The lesson planning procedure which follows is a succinct method of quickly attaining tenable rationale for decisions related to each of the above facets of instruction (content, methods, materials). There is no guarantee that the defensibility of the rationale will always be upheld. However, the likelihood of a teacher's successfully defending himself against a charge of bias or inappropriateness in decision-making concerning these areas will be significantly better if he has thought through his reasons for his decisions, than if he has not thought through them!

Defending Your Decisions Before They're Challenged

Each question below should be asked during the planning phase of any lesson.

Instructional Planning Guide

1. What are the main things I want my students to *remember* relative to this topic?
2. *Why* do I want my students to remember this?
3. How can I *best* help my students to remember it?
4. What are the main things I want my students to be able to *do* when they complete this unit of study?
5. Which speaking/writing/listening/reading skills do I want to develop?
6. How will I *state the assignment* to the class?
7. Which *materials* need to be made available to students for independent study?
8. When will my *help* be most needed by the student?
9. *How* and *for what purpose* will I evaluate the student's work?

Let's look at an item by item discussion of the *Instructional Planning Guide*. Remember that there are two main purposes for using the *Guide*. First, you naturally want to prepare and present the best lesson possible and with the best materials available. Second, and equally important, you want to be able to defend your decisions should a challenge arise from any group or individual concerning any of your instructional decisions.

The questions in the *Instructional Planning Guide*, if answered thoroughly by you, should enable you to easily and readily accomplish both of these objectives each time you teach a lesson. This is true whether you complete an extensive written lesson plan, or whether you merely think through each question and are prepared to respond to any challenge which might arise.

1. *What are the main things I want my students to remember relative to this topic?* This question assumes that you know exactly what you want your students to master in the way of content knowledge. The best way to specify this is in the form of a behavioral objective. What you should ask yourself is, "What do I want my students to know when they walk out of my classroom that they did not know when they entered my classroom?"

If the content you are presenting is not new content, then the question can be rephrased, "What do I want my students to know better when they walk out of my classroom that they did not know as well when they walked into my classroom?" The reason for this question is that ultimately a teacher will find himself or herself in a situation in which a parent or a superior will ask the teacher to specify exactly what it was that he was trying to teach in his or her classroom. It is amazing how often teachers cover content with only a vague or general notion of what it is they are trying to get across. General answers such as, "I'm trying to teach American History," or, "I'm trying to teach some underlying principles of the population explosion," will usually not suffice as an adequate response to a client or a superior bent on creating problems for a teacher. It is desirable for a teacher to specify precisely the fact or concept he or she intends for the students to master. Imagine the embarrassment if you were asked exactly what you wanted your students to know, and you could not answer the question after having spent several class periods on a general topic. Not only would you be in an indefensible position professionally, your position would also be indefensible in terms of your accountability to your students. A teacher who does not know exactly what he or she is shooting at will never hit the target.

The preceding comments on specific objectives may seem to

be totally unnecessary or superfluous. However, after having spent countless hours in numerous classrooms ranging from kindergarten through the college level, the authors can assert unequivocally that, too frequently, lessons are conducted because they happen to appear in a textbook, or because, "That's what has always been taught." As an aside, it might be added that many independent study assignments lead students to the point of frustration because teachers have failed to specify exactly what it is they would like their students to learn as a result of the assignment.

2. *Why do I want my students to remember this material?* A natural question following the first question of *what* do I want my students to remember is the question of *why* a teacher has chosen specific content to be remembered. Parents' rights activists in the '80s have been appalled to discover, for example, that one social studies textbook included an eight page discussion of Marilyn Monroe with only one page devoted to World War II. The teacher who used this social studies material without really considering what it focused upon would have great difficulty defending his students' mastery of trivia to the exclusion of an in-depth study of one of the major events in the history of mankind. Not only is it important, then, to specify exactly what it is that you want your students to know, you should have a good reason why you want your students to know or to master particular information.

The reason is simple. With many diverse groups striving for pre-eminence, or fighting for the survival of their basic values in our pluralistic American society, it is almost impossible to focus on the mastery of any content without offending one group or another. The best defense for selecting content can be found in a school district curriculum guide. Curriculum guides which give specific objectives or which delineate specific content, provide the teacher with a built-in defense against allegations of bias or poor judgment in selecting content. Where there is no specific set of objectives in a district curriculum guide, other satisfactory defenses for the selection of content include the potential social utility of the content (i.e., the likelihood that students will need to have mastered particular content to survive in society); the fact that content is reflective of a contemporary problem which could affect students as children or as future citizens, or the selection of content which provides foundational knowledge upon which future advance mastery of the subject can be built. Of course, these are not the only reasons for the selection of content. The important fact to remember is that a teacher should *always* have a rationale for selecting specific content to be mastered by students.

3. *How can I best help my students to remember this material?* The importance of the judicious selection of methodology or materials can perhaps best be illustrated by this true story. A junior college journalism instructor decided to teach his students what it is like to "live on the edge as a writer." To accomplish this objective, he walked into class one day with a real revolver. He was the only one who knew the revolver was not loaded. He looked at the students and then placed the revolver to his head as though he was about to commit suicide. In front of his horrified students, he pulled the trigger. Of course, nothing happened, and he then went on to explain what his purpose was in performing his mini-dramatization. Understandably, some of his students were traumatized; several horrified students complained to the administration of the junior college. The professor received a severe reprimand because of the inappropriateness of his methodology. Was the method effective? Obviously! Was it appropriate? Obviously, it was not. The best method, then, for getting information across to students may not always be the most appropriate method.

Again, parents' rights groups are increasingly aware of methodology used in the public schools. For example, in one of the larger school districts in Colorado, parents became incensed when an elementary teacher employed methods of teaching children which, in the parents' opinion, had "an occult religious basis." The parents raised a challenge to the teacher's methods. At this writing, the teacher has won a suit against the parents claiming that, among other things, the parents slandered her.

In West Virginia a high school teacher was charged with contributing to the delinquency of a minor as a result of activities by students attempting to complete a science assignment. The teacher was running a contest designed to help students learn about skeletal structure. According to the Associated Press report, the teacher "promised to award points toward a grade to students who brought in bones on a list he posted. The list included foxes, cows, monkeys, and humans. The human entry was followed by an asterisk with the warning 'at your own risk.'" The Associated Press story went on to say that human bones were listed as worth far more points than any other bones. One of the science teacher's students, a fifteen-year-old boy, decided to "bring in the bones of a woman who died in 1935 and who was buried in the local cemetery." It is difficult to tell exactly what the teacher's thinking process was in creating the assignment. Perhaps the teacher was merely in a lighthearted frame of mind and intended to be funny. Had the teacher followed the planning procedure under discussion on these pages, though, he would not have made a mistake which proved to be so potentially damaging to his career.

Any discussion of methodologies will ultimately address the question not only of whether the methodology is the most effective for conveying the information to students, but it will also include the question of whether the methodology is the "*most appropriate* methodology" or "the *only* methodology" which can be effective in achieving the objectives of the lesson. The same test applies to the selection of methodology as the test concerning the selection of materials. It is a simple one:

- Are these the only materials available, or is this the only method available that is absolutely the most effective set of materials or the most efficacious method for pursuing the goals of instruction?
- Are the methods and materials likely to violate basic values,

beliefs, interests, or concerns of any of the students in my classroom?

It is not recommended that teachers abandon what they feel to be legitimate and justifiable methods or materials. It is, however, extremely likely that for any given objective, there are multiple methods and a wide variety of materials available to achieve the teacher's goal. Energy expended in defending oneself against allegations concerning the injudicious or inappropriate selection of methods or materials can be better expended in providing quality alternatives which reflect sensitivity to the diverse populations represented in any given classroom.

4. *What are the main things I want my students to be able to do when they complete this unit of study?* Not all lessons are product oriented. Some are process oriented. In the case of a process oriented assignment, the teacher has as his or her focus certain skills or abilities that the student should be able to demonstrate upon completion of the unit of instruction. In situations in which it is difficult to answer question 1 above, it should be possible for the teacher to provide an answer to question 4. Lessons can be either product oriented, process oriented, or values oriented. A teacher can generally defend his reason for selecting product oriented or process oriented objectives. But the area of values oriented objectives is fraught with hazards and pitfalls since there is so little agreement today on what constitutes a set of values acceptable to all elements of society. Witness, for example, the controversy in the late '80s surrounding sex education classes and whether information about condoms should be made available to third grade students, or whether sex information clinics has a proper place on the high school campus without addressing the concomitant of values such as abstinence and birth control. If a teacher feels led to enter an area of controversy as a part of his classroom instruction, one defense which can be used for selection of methods or materials is that in order to enable his students to do certain things in society that responsible citizens should be

doing (such as writing letters to the editor, responding to editorials on television, or becoming active in civic organizations or other organizations), it is necessary to have students address controversial issues in controversial forums. Once again, the most important thing to remember is that the teacher should have thought through specifically what he wants the students to be able to do and *why* his objectives are justifiable.

5. *Which speaking/writing/listening/reading skills do I want to develop?* In one sense it can be said that this question can cover a multitude of "sins." That is to say, it would be possible to justify virtually any assignment or any activity on the basis that specific writing/listening/reading/speaking/thinking skills are being elicited. For example, to produce a critical thinker or to produce someone who can clearly articulate a position on complex or controversial issues, one must provide the learner with the opportunity to think critically through the process of analyzing propaganistic materials or through delving into what are obviously biased source materials. Any good college textbook in the area of reading instruction will identify a comprehensive list of critical reading, critical thinking, and advanced rhetoric skills. Few educators would argue with the contention that the ability to listen, speak, read, write, and to critically address complex issues is essential to maintain a free society. One readily apparent and legitimate defense a teacher can use in his selection of objectives, methods, or materials is an argument based upon the development of advanced communication skills.

The teacher should expect, however, that any special interest group might come forward with material which could be used for the development of critical, receptive and expressive communication skills. At the risk of appearing redundant, the main point is that the teacher should be able to defend his instructional decisions and that the development of advanced critical, expressive and receptive communication skills constitutes a tenable rationale for such decisions.

6. *How will I state the assignment to the class?* Most experienced teachers know that one of the most common questions raised in any class is the question, "What were we supposed to do?" accompanied by a look of consternation on the face of a puzzled student. Teachers also know that most telephone calls from student to student in the evening hours (that is, when they concern homework) are related to "What did he want us to do?" Sometimes the situation becomes more serious than an inquisitive exchange among students. Students may become frustrated when attempting to explain to their parents what an assignment was. Often they totally misrepresent the assignment and the teacher in the process. Irate parents then contact the school, the principal, or other parents to complain about the teacher, the assignment, or anything else related to their child's apparent frustration. There can be little misunderstanding of assignments or a teacher's comments, if the teacher thinks through the assignment ahead of time and provides the assignment *in writing* for the student. Many unpleasant client/ teacher confrontations could be avoided by the simple expedient of a written assignment which includes the following components: *a)* the objective of the assignment; *b)* a purpose for the assignment stated in a way that will show both students and parents the ultimate outcome. (In other words, what's in it for the student?); *c)* materials needed for the assignment; *d)* the form in which the assignment should be submitted; and *e)* the criteria for grading the assignment. While it is unlikely that a teacher would face litigation as the result of a poorly stated assignment, it is possible that a teacher could face criticism and undesirable or unpleasant confrontations with students, parents, or administrators as a result of his failure to provide clearly understandable instructions. Following item 6 on the instructional planning guide can help a teacher avoid such undesirable outcomes.

7. *Which materials need to be made available to students for independent study?* A concerned teacher will attempt to address the specific needs and beliefs of all of his students. The October

24, 1986 ruling in Greenville, Tennessee ordered the public school system to excuse children from reading books their parents find objectionable, and permitted parents to teach reading to their children at home. It is logical, therefore, to conclude that a desirable course of action on the part of the teacher will be to provide a wide variety of instructional materials to his students.

Of specific concern to Christian teachers has been the extent to which they can use Christian oriented materials in the public school classroom. In 1986, *Liberty Magazine* published an article entitled, "A Liberal Case for Religion in School" by Warren A. Nord. The synopsis of what the courts specifically and presumptively permitted is excellent.

Dear Teacher:

The Bible—you know, that Book you've been hiding in the library safe—take it out. Read it to your students. You can even whisper a prayer on the way to the classroom. (Or shout it, for that matter, though shouted prayers might not be considered in good taste by conservative school boards.) The point is, no black-robed Supreme Court justice, with or without horns, will be lurking around a judicial corner to hale you into court for violating the First Amendment.

Perhaps no decisions in court history have been so misunderstood as the so-called prayer and Bible-reading decisions. Lawyers look them up under the headings of *Engel v. Vitale*, 370 U.S. 421 (1962) and *Abington School District v. Schempp*, 374 U.S. 203 (1963).

In neither case was God "expelled" from the public schools.

The Court did not prohibit recognition of God in public life.

Officeholders paid by tax funds can still invoke God, mother, and the Bible.

Here is what the Court really called unconstitutional:

1. Requiring the recitation of a non-sectarian prayer as part

of a religious exercise.

2. Requiring the reading of a portion of the Bible or the recitation of the Lord's Prayer as part of a religious exercise.

Activities Specifically Permitted

The following activities were found to have no constitutional restraint:

1. Use of the Bible as a reference work for the teaching of secular subjects.

2. Use of the Bible as an instrument for nonreligious moral inspiration.

3. Study of the Bible for its literary and historic qualities.

4. Objective instruction of comparative religion or the history of religion and its relationship to the advancement of civilization.

5. Reciting historical documents (such as the Declaration of Independence) that contain reference to God.

6. Singing officially espoused anthems that include the composer's profession of faith in God.

7. Patriotic or ceremonial references to God.

Activities Presumptively Permitted

In addition, Justice Brennan, in a concurring opinion in the *Schempp* case, indicated that the following activities were constitutionally permissible:

1. Providing churches and chaplains at military establishments and in penal institutions.

2. Exempting ministers and divinity students from military service.

3. Excusing children from school on their respective religious holidays.

4. Providing temporary use of public buildings to religious organizations when their facilities are unavailable because of emergency.

5. Saying invocational prayers in legislative chambers by mature adults who may absent themselves from such cere-

monial exercises without incurring any penalty, direct or indirect. [2]

It can be seen that a teacher has wide latitude in selecting materials, but a teacher should also be sensitive to the possibility of offending the parents of his students by subjecting their most basic belief systems even to what can be called "objective scrutiny."

8. *When will my help be most needed by the student?* It is highly unlikely that a legal challenge would be raised against a teacher for not adequately helping a student in the process of pursuing an independent assignment. It *is* likely, however, that abundant criticism could be directed toward a teacher if a student ran into difficulty in completing such an assignment. Experienced teachers know that often they are the victims of parental anger when the frustrated child is incapable of completing assignments. Teachers are blamed for inadequately preparing pupils to do the assignment or for not preparing them at all. The result is predictable and inevitable: a confrontation requiring energy and time on the part of the teacher to explain why the student was unable to complete the assignment, and emotional stress in anticipating the complaints of parents or in engaging in a hostile conference. While the teacher's rights, as such, are certainly not under attack, the teacher's reputation and peace of mind are. The best thing a teacher can do to head off such undesirable results is to anticipate whether and when the student will need help and to make himself available to the student for such help. The written assignment identified in item 6 above is a good place for the teacher to indicate his availability to the students. Both his indication of availability and his actual availability will enable him to avoid the unpleasant results which inevitably occur when students encounter obstacles in independently pursuing their work.

9. *How and for what purpose will I evaluate the students' work?* Few aspects of the public school have come under as much attack in the past, and promise to continue under attack in the

future, as the area of evaluation and grading of students' work. Often a grade can mean the difference in a student's securing a generous scholarship or other stipends for continuing study. In lower grades, the teacher's assignment of a grade to a student may be interpreted by some parents as a reflection upon them and upon the child's total ancestry! No other area of a teacher's experience provides as many possibilities for vulnerability as the area of evaluation and grading.

How can you best protect yourself against criticism or litigation when it comes to evaluating pupils' work? First, a well-defined set of criteria for evaluation should be spelled out and should be available to students and to their parents for every assignment, activity, or unit which will be graded by you. Second, you should be clear as to what the purpose of your evaluation is. Will you use the evaluation to guide the student to further study or to correct deficiencies? Will you use the evaluation to place the student in a particular course or program of study? Will you use the evaluation to report the student's progress to the parents?

The authors believe that criterion referenced evaluation is usually more defensible than norm referenced evaluation. This means, simply, that the student is evaluated against a criterion of performance rather than on a basis of how he compares to the particular group in which he finds himself.

The best defense against the charge of prejudice, arbitrariness, or capriciousness in grading students' work is an evaluation system which demonstrates a direct relationship between the teacher's expectations and the teacher's specified objectives. If specific criteria are spelled out ahead of time; if these criteria are made available to students, and if these criteria are clear, the teacher has laid a solid foundation for any potentially necessary defense of his decision-making process or of his decision itself as it relates to evaluating a student's work.

Summary

It is not always possible to anticipate potential pitfalls as a teacher attempts to teach a class with a wide diversity of values, belief systems, and basic needs. The increasing militancy of both the left side and the right side of the political spectrum necessitates a new attitude on the part of teachers which was not required of teachers of past decades. Specifically, teachers need to be aware of the potential for criticism and even litigation brought against them for their decisions. The instructional planning guide presented in this chapter, along with the accompanying discussion addressing each of the items in the guide, is not a panacea. But it can be of valuable assistance to teachers in avoiding potential difficulties while carrying out their multifaceted professional tasks.

FOOTNOTES

[1] *Rocky Mountain News*, April 10, 1987, p. 50.
[2] *Liberty Magazine*, November-December, 1986, p. 13.

Chapter 7

How to Handle Difficult Parents: The Ten Commandments of Responding to Criticism

We were sitting in the faculty lounge. It was not a good place to cry. But the pressure—and the need to talk—had been the catalyst for Mrs. S. to pour out her problem, and the tears had just come. Dabbing at her eyes with a crumpled tissue, and trying to look as normal as possible whenever another teacher entered and then hastily left the lounge, Mrs. S. bared her hurt.

"I've been teaching for 23 years," she murmured, "and I have never encountered such hostility. Back-to-school night is usually just routine. I explain to the parents what the children are doing, answer a few questions, and socialize. I was caught totally unawares," she sobbed. "It was like an ambush, and I didn't know what to do. I haven't had a good night's sleep in two weeks, and I feel this tremendous anxiety . . . . " Her voice trailed off, and the tears continued, unabated.

What surprised me about the situation was that I hardly knew Mrs. S., but since her principal had caved in to parental pressure and had failed to back her, she had had nowhere else to turn for support.

What had happened? An inexperienced teacher had taken over the kindergarten class the previous year. She had failed to take the children through the reading readiness program. Now, it was November of first grade, and instead of demonstrating their proficiency in reading happy little pre-primer stories, the first graders in Mrs. S.'s class were being taught the basic readiness skills they should have had in kindergarten. Since the kindergarten teacher had given the parents glowing reports the previous year about the children's progress, there was now a consensus on their part that Mrs. S. was to blame for the fact that their children were not keeping up with the Joneses—i.e. other first graders of other parents in other schools. And the parents had vented their frustrations in a group setting at back-to-school night in Mrs. S.'s classroom. At first it had been in the form of thinly-veiled accusations, and then in overtly hostile references to Mrs. S.'s level of competence. And Mrs. S. had reacted normally. She had become flustered, she confessed. She had been unable to control the quaver in her voice, and the harder she tried to retain her composure, the worse she had looked. She most definitely would not commiserate with other teachers on the staff, and her principal, nearing retirement, would not back her up; so she was unconsciously seeking support from the visiting university professor.

Mrs. S.'s experience is an all-too-familiar story. Teachers present a symbol of authority that can be attacked with seeming impunity by parents who may be using the teacher for catharsis, as an outlet for frustration, hostility, or aggression which cannot be vented in the home, on the job, or in society at large. Often, parents, who themselves are responsible for their children's poor academic performance, their irresponsibility, or their uncontrolled and uncontrollable behavior, unconsciously seek a convenient scapegoat for their own failures. Their child's teacher nicely fills the bill. Teachers who are not tenured, or who are otherwise vulnerable to attack because of weak administrators who will not come to their defense, suffer tremendous anxiety and stress as they face hostile and sometimes less-than-rational clients. The cliche that people who enter the "helping" professions are "nice" people has a basis in fact. Many teachers are neither personally disposed nor professionally prepared to effectively respond to hostile audiences or to emotionally loaded parent-teacher conferences. The results of an ineffective response are detrimental not only to the teacher as a professional, but also as a person, and the detriment invariably creates additional unwitting victims: the teacher's pupils.

Several factors should be kept in mind, however, in thinking about parent-teacher conferences, back-to-school nights, or any other arrangements designed to encourage communication between the school and the home. First, parents have a right to know how their child is doing in school. They have the right of access to their child's records, and they have a right to receive courteous and honest answers to their questions. Within reasonable limits, often determined by school policy or by district guidelines, they have a right to visit their child's school and to observe in their child's classroom. Most parents are responsible and courteous in exercising these rights. And, although few teachers enjoy parent-teacher conferences, most teachers would agree that, for the most part, this facet of their job is not excessively unpleasant.

Unfortunately, an inescapable occupational hazard in the teaching profession is the confrontational parent conference. And it is this type of conference that can lead to professional and legal pitfalls for teachers.

This chapter will focus on how to respond to a hostile audience, whether it be an "ambush interview" in a group situation, or a private parent-teacher conference with implicit or explicit undertones of conflict. The techniques presented will help prepare concerned teachers to respond with dignity and with confidence to even the most inconsiderate and abusive of clients. These techniques are listed below in the form of *"The Ten Commandments of Responding to Difficult Parents."* A discussion of how each "commandment" protects your personal and professional rights follows the list.

THE TEN COMMANDMENTS OF RESPONDING TO DIFFICULT PARENTS

1. Thou shalt not answer non-questions.
2. Thou shalt not accept "ambush" appointments.
3. Thou shalt not provide information beyond what thou hast been asked for.
4. Thou shalt not make comparisons between pupils.
5. Thou shalt ask for restatements of questions when necessary.
6. If thou art about to lose thy cool, thou shalt leave the conference until thy emotions art under control.
7. Thou shalt retain thy professional dignity. (Thou shalt not answer insult for insult.)
8. Thou shalt not participate in "group" conferences by thyself. Thou hast no silver bullets; thou art not the Lone Ranger.
9. Thou shalt document all thy decisions and assertions.
10. Thou shalt not "put down" thy colleagues. Thou lowerest thyself when thou bendeth over to push others down. Thou shalt not put thyself down either. Thou didst thy best.

Using the "Commandments" to Protect Your Rights

Let's look at the "commandments," or techniques, one-by-one and determine how each technique can be of help in protecting a teacher's rights.

1) Thou shalt not answer non-questions. Almost every teacher has had the experience of having a parent make a comment similar to one of these. "My child hates school this year. I just don't know what to do with him. He gets a headache every morning." Or, "I think you should be spending more time on more important things in your classroom. My child seems bored most of the time." Notice that none of these statements constitutes a question. Each statement is an accusation. For a

teacher to respond would be foolish. In the first place, you have no idea what the parent's major concern is. You might respond to what you think the specific complaint to be, and discover, to your dismay, that you have answered a question which was not asked. In the process, you may provide a hostile parent with additional ammunition to continue attacking your professional competence, or, even worse, you as a person.

So how do you respond to a non-question? The best thing to do is to sit patiently and listen to the parent without responding at all. That's right—you just sit quietly and look at the parent attentively and respond with silence. The situation will probably be uncomfortable, but you will have to "tough it out." If you wait long enough, the parent will elaborate upon his or her original assertion. If the elaboration is still a non-question, you are not obligated to respond. You should continue to sit and wait patiently until a question is asked. If no question is asked and if there is a period of dead silence which becomes unbearably uncomfortable, it is appropriate for you to say, "Do you have a specific question you would like me to answer?" At that point the parent will either have to ask you a specific question or answer, "No." In either case you will be better off for having waited because the question will no longer be implied. It will be specific enough for you to provide a thoughtful answer.

The point of the first commandment is this: You have a right to expect that if you are to answer a question, a question should be asked of you. You have a right not to answer an accusation. You have a right to have the opportunity to address a specific question with a judicious and prudent response. It is impossible to respond judiciously and prudently to a vague, implied question hurled at you in the form of a hostile allegation which impugns your professional ability.

An additional factor ought to be kept in mind when considering a response to questions. It is important to recognize the *type* of question the parent is asking you. If you are in a group situation, it is possible that a parent may be asking an "esteem" question. An esteem question is one for which an individual is not really seeking an answer from you or from the person conducting the meeting. Rather, the person is trying to attract attention as a concerned parent, as an intelligent client, or as someone bold enough to ask the question. If you feel that an esteem question is being asked and that the person is not really seeking information, the best response to this type of question is to acknowledge the significance of the question, or the person's candor, forthrightness, or contribution to the dialogue of the group. If the question is a legitimate question for which the person is sincerely seeking an answer, you can be sure that the question will be restated by that person or by someone else.

It is also important to recognize a question which is a *hostile* question. The hostile question is sometimes couched in the form of an allegation or non-question discussed above. Occasionally, the hostility can be sensed by the teacher from the tone of the individual posing the question. In such a situation, it is desirable to ask for a restatement of the question. Some teachers have successfully responded to such questions by eliciting an elaboration of the question with the words, "You seem to be quite concerned," or, "I see this issue is an emotional one for you." Such a response quickly cuts through to the heart of the matter. This response, however, would not be desirable in a group situation, for it might only serve to unleash a barrage of hostility by people emboldened by the presence of a group. It is, however, an excellent question or response in a one-on-one situation involving parents and teacher.

A third type of question to identify is the question which is posed in a genuine quest for information. This question, which has no aura of hostility and no attempt to elicit esteem, should be answered directly, succinctly, and honestly.

As a teacher, you have the right to expect information seeking questions which are within the realm of your capabilities to answer. You have a right not to respond to questions which are hostile, which are designed to gain esteem for the questioner, or which have as their primary purpose the intent to put you down or to question your professional competence.

2) *Thou shalt not accept "ambush" appointments.* In the television news media there is a type of interview called the ambush interview. Basically, a news reporter, who may have been unable to secure a scheduled interview, waits for a moment when he can "catch" the proposed interviewee unaware and throw a question at him. The hope is that the latter will respond with an answer which might be more candid or more revealing than it would have been had he had time to consider a response. Admittedly, most parents will not schedule an "ambush" interview solely for the purpose of tripping up a teacher. However, despite the absence of hostile intentions, parents frequently employ the "ambush" interview technique quite by accident.

For example, picture this scene: A teacher is grocery shopping on a Friday evening. She is getting ready to have an adult discussion group at her house, and she is in a hurry after school to pick up a few treats to serve to the group. She is trying to get out of the supermarket and to get home to get everything arranged. Just as she is about to leave the bakery section along comes Mrs. Concerned Parent. Now Mrs. Concerned Parent may very well be one of the nicest people around. She probably is, and Mrs. Concerned Parent may not even realize that she is imposing upon the teacher's free time. So Mrs. Concerned Parent pops the question. "Hi," she says, "How are you? Say, Becky seems to be having a lot of problems in math, and I was wondering whether she has shown any improvement lately in her multiplication tables. Her dad and I have been helping her at home."

Now remember that the teacher has her mind on the adult discussion group coming to her house. She wants to hurry home and get everything prepared. She has had a long day, and it is a Friday afternoon. She also does not want to get engaged in a long conversation in the supermarket in the bakery section about Becky, or any other students for that matter. So she gives a "throwaway" response. "Just fine," she says, "I think she's shown great improvement. She seems to be doing quite fine." And with that the teacher says, "Nice seeing you," heads for the cash registers, and wends her way home.

Unfortunately, that's not the end of the story. Two weeks later the teacher, who by now has totally forgotten the casual "ambush," or what, to the parent, was a parent-teacher conference in the supermarket, is in a formal parent-teacher conference with the parent who accosted her. The teacher is in the process of describing how Becky does not seem to have made as rapid a progress as she should have made on her multiplication tables.

"What!" the parent exclaims in an irate tone of voice, "why, you told me just two weeks ago that . . . ," and you can finish the rest of the sentence. What should have been a pleasant parent-teacher conference, and what would have caused no problems whatsoever in communication between the parent and the teacher, has now become confrontational. Why? Because the teacher accepted an ambush interview. The teacher, who had no bad intentions whatsoever, responded to a parent who also had no bad intentions whatsoever. But the teacher, being pre-occupied and in a setting which was not the one in which she was accustomed to discussing school problems, responded inappropriately.

The point seems clear: to protect your rights and to protect yourself as a professional, the best response to even the most benign "ambush" is a response like, "Thanks for asking. I'm glad you're interested. If you would like to call the school, I'll check the records so that I can be precise in my answer. Have a nice day." If you follow that type of response, you cannot spontaneously respond with words you will later regret, and no one can accuse you of being hostile, unfriendly, or uncooperative because your response does promise that you will conduct the interview in a professionally controlled setting.

3) *Thou shalt not provide information beyond what thou hast been asked for.* The importance of this commandment can

be best illustrated by the following story.

A neophyte attorney was defending his first client against charges of drunken driving. He had carefully built his case. He could sense success, and he was moving in for the final coup. On the witness stand was the arresting officer. The attorney eagerly approached his final series of questions. "Tell me," he asked in the most innocent tone of voice, "are you the arresting officer?"

"Yes, I am," replied the officer.

"And when you arrested my client, you were sure that he was drunk?"

"Yes, I was sure," replied the officer.

"Did you give him a sobriety test?" the attorney asked.

"No, I did not give him a sobriety test," the officer responded.

"Hmm," said the attorney, "tell me then, did you give him a breathalyzer test?"

"No, I did not," the officer replied.

"I'm curious," the attorney said with a disdainful look at the officer and an appealing look to the jury, "how did you determine that my client was drunk?"

"Well," the officer replied slowly, "I used my experience. I looked at him and he certainly looked drunk to me."

"You didn't give him a sobriety test? You didn't make him take a breathalyzer exam? And you nevertheless arrested him for drunk driving on the basis of your experience in determining that people are drunk?"

"That's right," replied the officer.

Now it was time for the kill. Straightening up and throwing his shoulders back, sensing that victory was imminent, the attorney incredulously declared: "On your *experience*! How long, sir, have you been a police officer?"

"Two months," replied the officer.

"Two months! That certainly isn't very much experience," the attorney replied.

At this point the attorney had won the case, but he could not resist punctuating his victory. Looking the officer right in the eye, and again appealing to the jury to participate in his derision of the officer's testimony, he haughtily asked, "On what, then, did you base your decision, if you had been a police officer for only two months? What kind of experience can you say you brought to bear in determining that my client was drunk?"

The officer's response was terse and destructive. "Fifteen years as a bartender before becoming a police officer."

The jury broke into spasms of uncontrolled laughter. The red-faced attorney returned to his client's side. He had said too much.

A similar situation often exists in parent-teacher conferences where a teacher is asked about a child and provides information beyond that asked. For example, a parent asks a question about a child's progress in science, an area which was previously marked down on the report card. The teacher responds, "Well, I have noticed progress in group work in science and that has pleased me greatly. Susan seems to be making more contributions; she seems less shy about participating, and the other children appreciate what she has to say." At that point, what the teacher said constitutes an adequate, honest response to the parent's question.

However, the parent doesn't respond immediately, and the teacher, being nervous, continues, "I certainly am glad to see that. After the trouble Susan had last week on the playground with Dennis and his friends, it makes me feel good to see that she has been accepted again by the group."

"Trouble?" responds the parent with deep concern, "what trouble? Susan didn't say anything about trouble." At that point the teacher recalls how happy she was to be able to help Susan with her problems and that she had remarked to herself at the time that it was a good thing that Susan's parents, who tended to overreact to any social problem, were not aware of the minor problem which was corrected at school. Now, however, the teacher has inadvertently opened up a whole new area, and what would have been a very satisfactory parent conference, now becomes a conference devoted to counseling and placating Susan's parents so that they do not impose their inordinate concerns upon their daughter who has already successfully dealt with the incident and has totally forgotten about it.

Teachers have also been known to attempt to mollify parents who are concerned about a child's poor performance in one area by exaggerating the child's skills and proficiencies in another area. While the mollification process works for that particular conference, it often comes back to haunt the teacher in a subsequent conference when the parents want to know why the child's promised skill level was never attained. This does not mean, though, that teachers should never discuss extra information with parents. Simply that some discretion may be necessary in the parent/teacher partnership.

4) *Thou shalt not make comparisons between or among pupils.* Some conferences can become quite uncomfortable because it may be difficult for a teacher to find much in the way of progress to share with parents. In fact, the teacher may do nothing but express one problem after another until the parents are showing deep concern, and the teacher senses that the parents are either going to become hostile, make allegations about the teacher to the principal, or go home to confront their child with his academic or social inadequacies. The teacher, wishing to defuse such undesirable consequences of an unavoidably honest conference, might offer a comment such as: "Yes, I know Randy seems to be doing poorly; however, you can see that he is doing a lot better than the child whose work this is." And though the teacher covers up the child's name, she shows another child's work which is even worse than poor Randy's. The only problem is, unbeknown to the teacher, the other child turns out to be Randy's cousin. The child's work is immediately recognizable by Randy's parents who report it to their nephew's parents. You can imagine the consequences.

On the other hand, a teacher may be having trouble persuading parents that their child's work is, indeed, of substandard quality. Almost every teacher has had the experience of encountering parents who are absolutely positive that their child is gifted, and that the level of their child's work deserves a much higher grade than the teacher has recorded. It is very tempting at that point for a teacher to say to herself, "All right, since I can't convince you of how poor your child's work really is, I am going to have to haul out my big guns." So the teacher pulls out some top quality work and sets it beside the substandard work of the child whose parents think he deserves an "A." The teacher thinks that the comparison ought to be obvious—that the parents will immediately see that their child's work is not deserving of a higher grade.

Unfortunately, usually what is obvious to the teacher is not obvious to the parents. If they could not see in the first place that the work was of substandard quality, then most likely they will not be able to accept that conclusion when faced with an uncomfortable comparison of their child's work with the work of another. And such a comparison could backfire. The parents could demand to see further comparisons of their child's work.

While parents do have a right to know how their own child is doing in school, they have no right to see the records of other children. A teacher who reveals the progress, test scores, and anecdotal records or data about other children is opening himself or herself to serious professional and/or legal difficulties. It is not necessary or desirable to make comparisons between or among pupils. Not only does this rule hold true in parent-teacher conferences, but good teachers know that each child should be treated as an individual and that each child's work and behavior should be dealt with in relation to what constitutes realistic expectations for that child based upon his particular personality and abilities.

5) *Thou shalt ask for restatements of questions when necessary.*

6) *If thou art about to lose thy cool, thou shalt leave the*

conference until thy emotions art under control.

Each of these commandments is related to a situation in which the parent-teacher conference, for some reason or another, becomes very uncomfortable for the teacher. A legitimate question may be asserted in a very uncomfortable fashion. The question may be one which the teacher cannot immediately answer because he/she did not anticipate it. The conference may deteriorate to the point where emotions are about to rumble to the surface and create a confrontational situation. It is never good to try to answer a question if you feel that you are rattled or that you cannot adequately respond. In this situation it is desirable to ask parents to restate the question. This will give you some time to think about an answer, and it might also put the question into a different perspective so that an immediate answer comes readily to mind. If the situation is such that the conference is not a pleasant one, and you feel yourself becoming upset to the point of crying or losing your temper, then it is time for some drastic action.

You may want to keep some information about your students in a place some distance from where the parent-teacher conference takes place. For example, you might keep some information about each student in the filing cabinet in the teachers' lounge or in the office. Why? If the conference becomes exceedingly uncomfortable and if it's impossible to hide that lump in your throat or the flush emerging on your cheeks, then you can say something like the following: "I'm sure that I can give you a better answer if I look for some information I have on file down the hall." Your statement is, indeed, true. You probably will be able to give a better answer if you leave the room to look at information on file elsewhere. Taking a trip down the hall will give you an opportunity to control the emotions which you know would only contaminate communication between you and the parents.

In Proverbs 12:23 (NIV) we are told, "A prudent man keeps his knowledge to himself, but the heart of fools blurts out folly." Anger tends to reveal itself in different ways with different people. However, one way in which anger consistently shows itself is in the lack of control of some emotion. The main purpose of asking for a question to be restated, or of leaving the immediate conference area is to regain control of one's emotions in order to ease the communication process.

7) *Thou shalt retain thy professional dignity.* If you look at the preceding two commandments and take the evasive maneuvers necessary until you can retain or regain your composure, you probably will not have too much of a problem following Commandment 7. Statements made by the parents may be statements that you can respond to with incisive countercomments.

Scripture provides some wonderful guidelines on responding to situations in which people are being aggressive. The Bible tells us that our attitude should be like that of Christ who, "When they hurled their insults at him, he did not retaliate" (I Peter 2:23, NIV). Maintaining your dignity as a professional will go a long way toward quenching the fires of passion that some bring to a parent-teacher conference. In fact, many times not only will the fires of passion go out, but your response, one of dignity, may elicit from parents concerns about a problem that has absolutely nothing to do with their child—a problem for which you might be able to provide help and counsel.

One other way to head off a confrontational situation is to "put the nail next to the hammer." What this means, simply, is that if you anticipate a confrontational conference, arrange the seating so that you are sitting next to the parents rather than across from them. It is very difficult to shout at someone or to engage in a head-to-head confrontation when you are seated right next to a parent, almost shoulder to shoulder, looking at a piece of material. The physical environment can go a long way toward defusing potentially explosive situations and toward helping you retain your professional dignity. You cannot be successfully accused of acting "unprofessional" if you do not act unprofessional. This means that you forego the opportunity to criticize the parents, their poor parenting skills, or the child's poor home environment. (This includes reminding them that if they would give their child breakfast, maybe he wouldn't come to school so cranky; or if they would see to it that he got to bed on time, he wouldn't be so hard to contend with every day; or if they accepted their responsibilities as parents, he wouldn't be a discipline problem; or if they wouldn't argue so much at home, he wouldn't be so argumentative at school.) Even if your statements are true, they will not help you to help the child. Nor will they enhance your professional dignity.

8) *Thou shalt not participate in "group" conferences by thyself. Thou hast no silver bullets. Thou art not the Lone Ranger.* There is certainly a difference between an informational meeting and a group conference. The former is designed to provide information to parents and to explain materials, methods, and curriculum. A conference, on the other hand, gets into specifics about the work of the child(ren), his behavior, or other facets of his performance in the school setting. In a group conference, many times parents, who otherwise would conduct themselves with deference to you as a teacher or with courtesy for you as a human being, will be emboldened to throw caution to the winds and become hostile and aggressive. There is a "pack syndrome" which seems to occur when parents who are frustrated by one thing or another have the opportunity for group catharsis. Too often teachers are victimized in this type of situation. It is never desirable to allow yourself to be placed in an adversarial relationship where you represent one side and a group represents the other side. This not only places you at a disadvantage in presenting your point of view, but you will also be at a total disadvantage if it is ever necessary to recount what happened during the meeting. If specific personal questions come up in a group, the best course of action is to ask parents to sign up for individual conferences and to conduct such conferences at your mutual convenience.

9) *Thou shalt be able to document thy decisions.* One of the best defenses against a challenge to your professional decisions

or to your professional judgment is solid documentation of the reasons underlying your actions. If you assign a child a certain grade for his work, you should have a good reason for your decision. The best defense against a charge of arbitrariness in grading, for example, is a well-developed set of criteria upon which all grading is based. This same "commandment" holds true in questions of discipline, decisions about content, methods, or materials in teaching, decisions on grouping for instruction, or in any other decision affecting the conduct of your classroom or the welfare of your students. You are the first line of defense in protecting your rights. Good record-keeping, samples of pupils' work, duplicates of correspondence, and published policies and procedures are important evidence against nuisance allegations, lawsuits, or the failure of a skittish administrative structure unwilling or unable to back up its teachers.

10) *Thou shalt not be defensive.* Any teacher worth the title is concerned when he fails to reach a pupil. There is a natural tendency to be defensive when pupils fail to respond. We feel that we are somehow responsible, even though we may point to external causes for a student's failures. It is important to remember, though, that even perfect teachers do not reach all of their students. The Lord Jesus Christ is the most striking example of that truth. Some, who knew better, obstinately resisted both His message and His methods. Others were simply not able to comprehend what He taught. Even those with whom He had extended contact were sometimes a disappointment to Him. They repeatedly misunderstood Him; they botched their assignments, or they failed to do them at all. (See Matthew 16:6, 19:13; Mark 9:18,32; Matthew 26:38-46.) Consider this: All of Jesus' disciples failed the mid-term exam (Gethsemane); one, Judas, failed the final.

The point is simple. If you did the best you could, you have no reason to be defensive, even if other teachers seem to be doing better. If a *formal* challenge is raised, your careful adherence to the preceding nine "commandments" will provide you with a good protection.

Summary

It is inevitable that teachers will face hostile audiences at some point. But difficult situations can be made worse, to the point of creating legal problems, if a teacher responds inappropriately. The "Ten Commandments" for defusing potentially explosive situations and avoiding potential legal difficulties, can be successfully followed by even neophyte teachers.

Chapter 8

Discipline: How Far Can You Go?

The governing of the classroom must be approached as an absolute, unlimited monarchy, with the teacher at its head. Only after absolute control has been established, can the teacher approach the task of instruction. [1]

The advice of the quotation above is certainly not advice asserted by the authors of this book. However, given the current state of discipline in the public schools, the advice would not be out of line. Although it became fashionable in American education during the 1960s and the 1970s to allow students considerable latitude to "do their own thing" in the classroom, experienced teachers were quick to realize that allowing too much latitude and too much freedom would ultimately lead to chaos, and that effective instruction could not take place in the classroom.

The quotation above is representative of the prevailing philosophy on discipline around the year 1800. That this philosophy would still be an effective philosophy today attests to the fact that children, if left to their own inclinations, will prove the truth of Proverbs 22:15, "Foolishness is bound up in the heart of a child." In other words, children need guidance and a structured environment, with very carefully defined rules to follow, in order to develop character and behaviors which will allow them to be considerate of others and to grow in wisdom and in knowledge.

Christian teachers, aware of the seriousness with which

Scripture treats the task of disciplining children, may not necessarily wince at the 1800s description of the classroom as "an absolute monarchy." Nevertheless, given the New Testament precepts outlined in Ephesians 6:1-4, perhaps the approach might be better described as a "benevolent dictatorship," in which the teacher assumes the responsibility for decisions affecting the discipline of children in the place of parents. Later in this chapter, though, the reader will discover that the authors advocate the participation of children in identifying rules and consequences governing the learning environment. Such participation is desirable from several points of view, not the least of which is that, when people have a part in making decisions affecting them, they are more likely to respond to direction within the constraints imposed by those decisions. The authors also believe that if children have an opportunity to participate in decisions affecting their behavior, it will lead to a development of self-discipline and self-control, the ultimate goals of any program of effective discipline. The fact, however, that children can participate in determining rules and consequences affecting classroom decorum does not mean that the teacher should abdicate responsibility to exercise final authority in deciding upon the appropriateness or inappropriateness of student behaviors or upon consequences affecting such behaviors.

Unfortunately, the climate of the 1960s and 1970s, which was a climate of permissiveness, was also a climate hostile to the exercise of authority. One problem shared by all teachers concerned with effective discipline was the failure of overprotective parents or cautious and anxious administrators who failed to back up teachers when they exercised disciplinary authority. For example, one teacher confided to the authors that at the beginning of a school year his principal advised the teachers in his school not to pursue discipline too vigorously lest the school encounter difficulties with parents. In response to a teacher's questions as to what they should do about discipline problems, the principal offered this advice: "Just try to ignore them." The result in this and similar situations was predictable: absolute chaos, or at the very least, classroom environments in which it was extremely difficult for teachers to teach and for students to learn.

This chapter will explore legal and practical considerations bearing upon the question of discipline in the public school classroom, with particular attention to teachers' legal rights and professional responsibilities in administering discipline. The practical suggestions given, if followed, should enable teachers to attain and to maintain effective control in the classroom, as well as to protect themselves against professional or legal challenges which might ensue as a result of errors of omission or commission.

Discipline: Some Actual Cases

Several years ago the Associated Press carried a story which told of an elementary principal who took what he described as a "destructive and uncontrollable" five-year-old kindergarten student to circuit court "for the child's own good." The story, emanating from Huntington, West Virginia, quoted the principal as saying, "I'm doing what I think must be done. I did it for his own benefit. The purpose is not to get at the child."

The attorney defending the child called the case "totally absurd," despite the fact that the child had been repeatedly charged with disruptive classroom behavior, and despite the fact that the child's parents had refused to take him out of the kindergarten program.

When asked to comment on the West Virginia case, most teachers are appalled that a principal would go to such lengths in a case involving a five-year-old. In this and in other cases in every public school in the country, one thing should be kept in mind. Teachers are responsible for the safety of *all* children. Principals, as the designated status authority in the local schools, are responsible for helping teachers carry out this mandate. It would, therefore, be inexcusable for a principal or for a teacher to allow a student to engage in disruptive and uncontrollable behavior if there was a substantial possibility of physical or emotional harm which could come to any other child in the classroom. In the absence of other means of controlling the child, and assuming that the principal had exhausted all of the school district's resources in attempting to control the child, it appears that the principal engaged in appropriate behavior. As drastic as the principal's action may seem, it would be even more drastic to have a child physically injured or emotionally damaged as a result of the school's failure to appropriately respond to a child whose behavior is out of control—regardless of the age of the child.

A first point to be made, then, about discipline is that drastic measures—as long as they are within the parameters prescribed and proscribed by state statute and district and local policy— are entirely appropriate in certain situations. Teachers have a responsibility to provide a safe environment, both physically and emotionally, in which children are able to learn without fear of other students' inability to conduct themselves in a civilized manner.

That such drastic action is not unusual is illustrated by a second case. On December 16, 1983, the *Greeley Tribune* carried an Associated Press story from LaJunta, Colorado. The story described a situation in which a 15-year-old girl was directed by the court to spend Christmas holidays confined at a state juvenile center where she had previously spent Thanksgiving break. The reason? The student had ignored a court order to attend school regularly. In this case, although the student's actions were not a threat to other students, the student's continuing disobedience of the law was a threat to the school district's authority and the school district's legal responsibility. Commenting on the case, the judge declared, "I'm determined you're not going to flaunt your disobedience of the orders of this court."

Under Colorado law compulsory school attendance falls under the domain of district courts. After the school's attendance officer issues a formal notice to offenders, they have ten days to begin regular school attendance. If the formal notice is ignored, both students and parents can be compelled to come to court. Drastic measures, it can be seen, are recognized by the courts as appropriate in situations in which flagrant violations of school regulations occur.

Even though such actions are available to schools, schools may not be, in the words of the court, "enclaves of totalitarianism." In 1969, in *Tinker v. Des Moines Community School Board* (393 U.S. 503) (Iowa, 1969), the Supreme Court declared, "School officials do not have absolute authority over their charges. The state may infringe on an individual's rights only when a material and substantial disruption of the ongoing program of the school is present. Mere apprehension of a disturbance is not a sufficient basis for a priority of denial of the right to communicate."

The information above is indicative of the quandary in which teachers have found themselves. On the one hand, they have been charged with maintaining an appropriate learning atmosphere and protecting the safety of all of their students. On the other hand, they have been told that they do not have absolute authority over children. The quandary is perhaps best summed up by M. Chester Nolte in an article entitled, "Discipline's Legal Consequences." It is a succinct summary of teachers' rights and teachers' responsibilities.

> ... *Students, being 'persons,' have certain constitutional rights which cannot be denied them under penalty of suit for damages. The Supreme Court ruled in* Wood v. Strickland *(95S. CT. 992.) (Ark. 1975.), that school 'officials' (which later courts have indicated also includes principals and teachers) may be held personally liable in damages 'if they know, or reasonably should have known, that what they were doing (depriving someone of a civil right) would result in a civil deprivation.* [2]

This opens the door to suits in such previously closed areas as peaceful assembly, right of privacy, freedom of the press and speech, and freedom of association. Nolte also points out that in 1975 the Supreme Court handed down due process guidelines to control suspension, expulsion, and corporal punishment. He concludes that, "When acting *in loco parentis* (or in the role of parent) to the child, a teacher must assume the role of child advocate, parent surrogate and protector of the child's rights, rather than the dangerous role of state agent out to collect evidence to punish a child." [3]

The point is clear. Disciplinary measures imposed upon students must take into consideration the rights guaranteed to them under the Constitution or by subsequent civil rights legislation. The problem emanating from the recognition of such a point is also clear. Since teachers have no way of knowing or, in some situations, even *anticipating* how certain disciplinary measures will be interpreted relative to the Constitution or to civil rights legislation, they would be wise to protect themselves by rigidly adhering to school district guidelines and to specific school policies in formulating disciplinary procedures and policies for their own classrooms.

Guidelines in Establishing Classroom Procedures

The information which follows can help establish specific classroom procedures that will protect the rights of teachers.

1. Familiarize yourself with school and district regulations. It is common procedure for school districts to have complete sets of guidelines available to all teachers. Beginning teachers, in particular, are given comprehensive packets of materials outlining everything from the district's personnel policies to curriculum directives and expectations for teachers as well as specific policies and procedures relating to more mundane matters such as field trips, extracurricular activities, and classroom discipline. It is an absolute imperative that a teacher familiarize himself with the district rules and regulations on discipline and adhere to them closely.

Where policies are unclear, the teacher should request, in writing, clarification of the specific policy or practice and retain a copy of the written request for his own files. The letter of request for clarification should include a section entitled "Desired Response." In it, the teacher should indicate that he wishes to receive *written* clarification by a specific date. In the event that district or school policies are ambiguous, hard to find, or for any other reason the teacher feels uncomfortable with their level of clarity, the teacher should make a formal request, again in writing, to appropriate administrators, requesting specific in-service sessions prior to the beginning of the school year which focus on the topics of discipline, teachers' rights, and their responsibilities. Even if a school district does not comply with a request for written clarification or for specific in-service sessions, you will have taken a major step toward protecting your rights by having a written record of the fact that you sought clarification on a specific date relative to specific policies.

2. It is important for teachers to establish, immediately upon entering a given classroom, control of the students. First day expectations should be put in writing. (Obviously, they should be cleared with the principal first and not deviate from school or district procedures.) When distributing first day expectations, the teacher should also know what he or she will do in the event that students violate any of the expectations. At this particular time, students do not need to know what the consequences will be. However, the teacher must so that she will not act extemporaneously in response to breaches of class rules. Such extemporaneous acts can create problems.

Immediately following the distribution of class rules and regulations on the first day, the teacher should seek to establish an appropriate rapport with the students. The authors recommend that teachers involve students in a discussion of what ought to constitute appropriate classroom decorum. From this activity, a list of appropriate and/or inappropriate behaviors can be given to students. The teacher should then put in writing a list of consequences which may follow the breaking of class rules. By giving students the list of rules and consequences, they are clearly apprised of both expected behaviors and anticipated consequences. However, the teacher should initiate the following step prior to such distribution.

3. A letter, similar to the one which follows, should be written by the teacher, cleared by the principal, and sent home to parents for their signature.

Dear Parents:

I am pleased to have your child, _____, as a student in my class this year. In order to attain a classroom atmosphere conducive to the best teaching and learning possible, the students and I have agreed upon the following rules:

1.

2.

3.

4.

5. (List rules agreed upon by teacher and students.)

In anticipation that some students may not always adhere to the rules, the following consequences for rule violations have been identified. One or more of these consequences may be imposed as a result of the violation of one or more of the rules.

1.

2.

3.

4.

5. (List consequences.)

Please review the preceding rules and consequences. If these rules and consequences appear to you to be appropriate for your child, please indicate your agreement with their appropriateness by signing your name in the space provided below. If you feel that the rules and consequences are not appropriate, please contact me by calling the school at (tel. no.) in order to make an appointment with the principal and me to discuss how you will ensure your child's appropriate behavior.

I am looking forward to working with you as a partner to provide for your child the best education possible.

Sincerely,

_____

(Your name)

_____

Parent's Signature

The reason for doing this is that, in the event that a specified discipline results in unanticipated, negative ramifications beyond the immediate consequence, the teacher has taken steps to protect himself. If parents agree that the rules and consequences are appropriate for their children, it will be difficult for them to assert, at a later time, that the teacher imposed unfair or injudicious rules or penalties upon their child. If, on the other hand, parents disagree with the rules and consequences, by making an appointment and discussing with the principal and the teacher their guarantee (which should be secured in writing by the principal and the teacher) of their child's behavior, they will have assumed a share of the responsibility in effecting a disciplinary program for their child. It would be difficult, in view of such an agreement, for the parents to claim injudicious, arbitrary, unprofessional acts on the part of the teacher, the principal, or the school.

4. Consequences should be selected to fit the child. In considering appropriate discipline for rule violations, two quotations come to mind: "There is nothing so unequal as the equal treatment of unequals," and "The same rule for the lion and the ox is oppression."

What this means, simply, is that in a public school setting, rule violations are not "crimes." The concept of "making the punishment fit the crime" is inappropriate. The teacher should consider the demands of fairness and justice to ensure that the consequence fits the particular *child*. The teacher should allow himself latitude in imposing consequences. Such latitude is provided when the teacher specifies in his letter to the parents that consequences *may* be imposed. Consequences should be perceived as a pool from which the teacher may draw in response to a specific incident or a specific child. A teacher should stay away from specifying specific consequences for specific rule violations as much as possible. From time to time it may be judicious to impose no consequence other than a verbal warning or reprimand to a student. The teacher can then honestly assert that a conscientious attempt has been maintained to address individual differences, not only in the instructional program, but also in the administration of discipline.

5. Think before you act. Although the question of spontaneous action or reaction has been addressed above, it is important to expand upon this point. All teachers can anticipate, at one time or another in their careers, outright defiance on the part of a student. One of the authors was present in a classroom when a student came in late and was told by the teacher to leave the room. "I don't have to leave the room, and you can't make me!" declared the student, assuming a posture of not only verbal defiance but also physical hostility.

The teacher was in an untenable situation. She could not back down in front of the class because to do so would be to surrender her authority. On the other hand, she was not big enough to physically remove the student from the classroom, and even if she could have, physically removing a student from the classroom is fraught with all kinds of potential legal hazards. Also, the teacher felt she could not leave the room to summon help because if, in her absence, another student was hurt by the defiant and hostile student, the teacher could be liable for damages. Nor could she send one of the students from her class because, in complying with the teacher's directive, the student would possibly incur the rejection and ostracization of the peer group. Worse yet, the second student might attempt to avoid the social repercussions of the peer group by also defying the teacher and compound the problem.

No matter what the teacher in the above situation chooses to do, the end result will be negative. Therefore, it is absolutely mandatory for teachers to determine ahead of time, with the principal's help, what they will do in cases of outright defiance. The procedure should be spelled out in writing and signed by appropriate school officials, attesting to the fact that the teacher has sought and received specific advice on what to do in such cases. If the written directive states that the teacher should leave the room to summon help, she has taken giant steps toward protecting herself against any subsequent charges of negligence should a child be hurt while the teacher is summoning help. No teacher should *ever* enter a classroom, under any circumstances, to teach a group of children without knowing ahead of time what he will do in the case of outright defiance by a student.

Neither should a teacher accept oral directives on what to do in cases of defiance. Written directives with appropriate signatures constitute the first line of defense in any legal or professional challenge to a teacher's rights. Indeed, in some districts teachers are *required*, as a part of their professional responsibilities, to prepare a list of rules and consequences which will be in effect in their classrooms. The suggestions above are not only appropriate in addressing specific district requirements, but they also constitute a judicious set of procedures in anticipation of any potential legal or professional challenge.

Specific Disciplinary Procedures: Their Legal Status

A variety of disciplinary actions have been upheld by the courts. It should be pointed out, however, that whether the courts, in future cases, would support any of the punishments or consequences discussed here would depend upon the circumstances under which they were imposed. Assuming, however, that the child's civil rights have not been abridged, and assuming that the teacher is acting in the best interests of all students to maintain a maximally effective teaching and learning environment, it is to be anticipated that the courts would uphold the rights of teachers to take the following actions:

1. In-school suspension in a specially designated area
2. Out-of-school suspension and/or expulsion, provided that comprehensive suspension, expulsion procedures and contingencies have been carefully spelled out, and that due process has not been violated. (The extent of due process that is required may depend upon the length of the suspension.)
3. Reasonable corporal punishment unless limited by state or local law or policy
4. Denial of extracurricular privileges
5. Keeping children after school
6. Physically restraining students (Teachers should be able to demonstrate that physical restraint was imperative to protect students from themselves or to protect other students from an unruly student.)

Undeniably, the imposition of certain consequences possesses greater possibilities for negative reactions on the part of the clients of the school than other consequences. Actions such as corporal punishment (spanking or otherwise inflicting physical pain), expulsion, suspension, denial of extracurricular activities, or reduction of grades can be anticipated as having the most potential for negative reactions from parents and from students. Serious consideration should be given to whether one wishes to impose consequences of this nature, except in the most extreme of cases. These measures are effective, but the stress incurred by teachers and public school administrators in defending themselves against attacks by angry parents can be avoided, when possible, through the imposition of less controversial disciplinary measures.

The whole question of rules, consequences, and disciplinary actions is a difficult one. If so called non-controversial consequences (ones which parents would not be likely to object to) are imposed, such as extra homework, denial of physical education or music activities, writing essays, or additional study problems to do, arguments are raised by educators justifiably concerned about using *academic* work as a punishment. Consider, for example, the counterproductivity of a teacher requiring a student to run laps for punishment when another teacher has encouraged children to engage in vigorous aerobic activity as a pleasurable pursuit. Or, consider the assignment of an essay as a punishment when the English teacher is attempting to instill the joy of writing. Disciplinary measures which are academic in nature should be avoided more than disciplinary measures which possess the potential of negative reactions from parents. The reason? The primary goal of teachers is to instill a love of learning, not to avoid controversy. Given a choice between selecting a consequence which would stifle the love of learning or one which would evoke controversy, the authors would side in favor of an action which might stimulate controversy but not extinguish the spark of the love of learning.

Summary

No teacher can teach without being able to maintain effective discipline. The free rein given to teachers in establishing "an absolute monarchy" in the 1800s has been restrained by court decisions upholding students' constitutionally guaranteed rights. Teachers must now be cognizant of those rights as well as of district and school policies bearing upon discipline in their classrooms. Teachers must, however, also maintain the safety of their students and an atmosphere conducive to learning.

Teachers can assert and protect their right to discipline by adhering to specific practices pertaining to discipline. Teachers can also protect their rights by providing in writing, through a letter to parents, an outline of the rules and consequences in effect in their classrooms.

Specific disciplinary practices which might be used, and which are legal, should be carefully weighed by teachers before imposing them upon students because of their potential for vigorous negative responses from the students or their parents. To avoid disciplinary actions which are likely to evoke a strong negative response or a legal or professional challenge to a teacher's rights, teachers should anticipate *ahead of time* which consequences they will impose, which behaviors they will or will not tolerate, and how they will respond in the event of flagrant violations of classroom behavior.

Teachers have a responsibility to protect their students. But they also have a right to protect themselves.

FOOTNOTES

[1] Camp, William G. "Problem Students Not New—Student Discipline Techniques, Circa 1800." *NASSP Bulletin.* Jan. 1981. Vol. 65, #441, pp. 40-44.
[2] Author updated version of *A Legal Memorandum* of the National Association of Secondary School Principals, May, 1976.
[3] *Ibid.*

Chapter 9

Teacher Evaluation:
Protecting Your Rights

"Almost a relief." That was a teacher's reaction following an action taken by a board of education and school district officials in a district near Denver, Colorado. The teacher had endured six months of close scrutiny by his principal and by supervisory personnel from central administration. The teacher had been observed 40 times between the beginning of the school year and the month of March by his school principal, and four times by an assistant superintendent of schools. The reason: Using inappropriate methods in the teaching process. School officials finally filed dismissal charges against him, initiating the first of a series of steps which could lead to the ultimate firing of the teacher.

Almost any teacher, experienced or inexperienced, will admit to some degree of stress when being observed by those who are in a position to evaluate his performance or who have been charged with the task of evaluating his performance. Teachers are well aware of the fact that philosophical differences concerning methods, the selection of materials, or nuances of teaching style may exist between supervisory personnel and the people they are charged to evaluate. Indeed, the term "philosophical differences" was precisely the term chosen to describe the difficulties between the teacher referred to above and his principal.

Given the fact of such philosophical differences, which are not only possible but more likely probable; add to that fact additional concerns such as continuing employment, reappointment, tenure, or in some cases, merit pay or desirable or undersirable transfers, and the whole question of evaluation of teaching performance is fraught with heavy, emotional undertones. Not even the most skilled teachers are immune to anxiety. Often these are the ones who have achieved the level of self-confidence and self-actualization which enables them to implement unorthodox teaching methods, to focus upon teaching objectives that are above mundane objectives, or to engage in creative teaching activities which may have the inadvertent or tangential result of "rocking the boat" of ideas, tradition, or teaching practices.

For example, let us assume that a Christian teacher has strong convictions about a particular contemporary issue. The teacher feels that it is a legitimate educational exercise to engage his students in public debate in a public forum. Let us assume, also, that that position is not specifically identified by the teacher in any way as "Christian." Nevertheless, the values reflected in the position can be clearly identified as having their origins in what can be construed as the "traditional Christian position." Let's assume, further, that the educational experience is outstanding. The students not only learn content, but in the process of learning content, they also develop the skills and abilities to articulate a position and to defend unpopular assertions. Even though the teacher has achieved specific objectives and can defend those objectives, philosophical differences pertaining not only to content in this case, but also to methodology, could have a negative result if the teacher's supervisor decided to evaluate the teacher at this particular time.

The result? An excellent teacher who can defend the methodologies and his position on the issue as well as his teaching objectives can nevertheless be threatened by hostile superiors. In short, the teacher can face the prospect of receiving an unfavorable evaluation.

Since even good teachers can be threatened by bad evaluations or by questionable evaluation procedures, it is critical that teachers be aware of their rights concerning the whole area of teacher evaluation.

Fundamentals of Education: What Every Teacher Should Know

There are basically two kinds of teacher evaluation: product evaluation and process evaluation. A third type of evaluation might be a combination of product and process evaluation. Let's take a look at each of these and examine, first, exactly what each one is; second, what the limitations of each are; and third, what the strengths of each type of evaluation are.

Product Evaluation. A product evaluation takes place when the outcomes of instruction are evaluated, and a teacher's strengths and weaknesses are determined on the basis of the extent to which the students have learned. Instruments used in product evaluation have included standardized tests and informal tests as well as discussions with pupils concerning what they may or may not have learned. Product evaluation is exactly what it implies: the evaluator looks at the final product and determines whether the teacher did, indeed, teach anything.

Product evaluation can be illustrated by the analogy of a fisherman. One could evaluate whether a fisherman is a good fisherman on the basis of whether he caught any fish. Regardless of how well the fisherman camouflaged himself, how artfully he was able to cast his bait where the fish might be lurking, or how beautifully and skillfully he was able to work the lure, if he caught no fish, he would be described as an unsuccessful fisherman. Conversely, a focus on a pure product objective would lead to the conclusion that a fisherman on his way home with a full stringer of fish was a good fisherman. The focus is on the product—the end result—rather than on how the person accomplished those results.

Let's take a look now at what problems might be encountered in a product-oriented teacher evaluation. We can do this easily by looking again at the analogy of the fisherman.

If we look strictly at the number of fish the fisherman caught, we can fail to see some important factors. Let's suppose that a fisherman went to fish in a lake that had just recently been stocked with hungry fish. The fish were circling, famished, looking eagerly for something to eat. The fisherman cast his bait on an old, rusty hook into the water. Immediately the fish converged on the bait, fighting one another to take it. The fisherman hardly had to do anything. The fish almost caught themselves. Is it right to conclude that the fisherman was a good one?

Now, take the case of another fisherman. This man went to a lake, and, seeing no one around, reached into his tackle box, removed a stick of dynamite, struck a match, ignited the wick, and flung the stick of dynamite into the middle of the lake. A massive explosion ensued. As the bubbles and ripples subsided, the bodies of fish began to float to the surface. Moving quickly, the fisherman gathered up all the fish and merrily made his way home. Would it be safe to conclude that this fisherman was a good fisherman, based solely upon his product and his efforts?

Let's look at a third fisherman. This fisherman went out and really didn't have too much up-to-date tackle. The place where he had to go to fish was usually crowded, and the fish had been spooked on numerous occasions. As the fisherman began to fish, there were frequent and significant distractions. His fishing was interrupted. He found that on several occasions, just as he was about to catch a fish, his equipment wouldn't work. He tried a number of different lures and a number of different retrieval methods, but nothing seemed to appeal to the fish, who had been exposed to virtually every fishing technique imaginable on numerous previous occasions. Overfed and distracted, these fish might not respond to even the latest revolutionary lure. Finally, however, after persevering diligently, the fisherman caught a couple of fish. Is it safe to conclude that this was a good fisherman?

The analogy of fishermen isn't far from the analogy of teaching. Fisherman #1 can be likened to a teacher who is assigned to a classroom where students are primed to learn.

They come from homes where education is valued. They have a hunger to discover new ideas. The teacher has the best of equipment and the best of circumstances in which to teach. Teaching is a pleasure, and the fish—or students—are highly responsive. The teacher has had a number of student teachers work under his supervision over the course of several years, and he reports that even the most bungling and neophytic attempts to teach have been met with success. The key? "Why it's the students," the teacher laughs. "Who couldn't succeed with such delightful kids as these?" Was the teacher a good teacher, or could anybody be a good teacher under these circumstances?

Let's look at example two. Here we can see that the fisherman achieved marvelous results. His methods were clearly unorthodox, though, and it doesn't take much close analysis to show that they could be exceedingly harmful. Similarly, there are teachers who can produce great results. Students *do* perform on tests; they demonstrate proficiency both on objective and subjective measures of achievement. But they may end up hating the teacher and the subject, developing a lifelong aversion to pursuing independent knowledge in that teacher's subject area. Yes, the teacher did make the students learn, but in the process, the teacher lost the students. It could be said that the teacher, like an army general, gained the objective but lost his troops. In education, however, there should be no such casualties. No product objective is worth turning a student off to a particular discipline, regardless of how proficient the student might become in it. What is the use of being able to give a virtuoso piano performance if one refuses to sit in front of a keyboard?

Let's look at fisherman #3 now. Fisherman #3 is the teacher who faces a classroom full of hostile or disinterested students. He might also have faulty equipment or lack materials. While he is trying to teach, he is distracted by the fact that there are many discipline problems or other adverse conditions under which he must work. One of those conditions might be an overcrowded classroom. Another might be the fact that his students have been exposed to teachers who could not persevere in such adverse circumstances, and who left the students at various times throughout the school year. Thus, these students are at a disadvantage, not only because education is not valued by their parents, or because they are laboring under adverse circumstances, or because they have been exposed to inadequate teachers and teaching practices in the past, but because, like fish who have been threatened too many times, they have developed a personal aversion to anything having to do with learning. Even the most appealing and alluring of motivational devices, educational experiences, or materials—even if they were available—fail to entice the students. What does happen, however, is that the teacher, through sheer determination, perseverance, and love is able to lift one or two students from the mire and give them the chance to blossom as fully productive citizens.

Which teacher is a good teacher? Which teacher deserves merit pay? Clearly, it can be seen that to focus only upon product outcomes in evaluating a teacher would be a serious mistake, and an indefensible evaluation procedure. Thus, if a teacher suspects that product measures will be used to evaluate him or her, the teacher ought to insist in writing that the other variables affecting product outcomes be considered in the evaluation process. This means that the teacher should (again, in writing) point out any adverse circumstances under which the teacher is laboring, including inadequate materials, inappropriate facilities, or inappropriate environments, underachieving students, students who are a discipline problem, inordinately high rates of absenteeism or truancy, lack of parental support, and other factors which have a bearing upon whether the teacher can do the job.

One additional example might point out how critical it is for teachers to bring these factors to light when they anticipate an evaluation focused on product objectives. One of the authors has had the experience of working with teachers in major metropolitan school districts, and of helping those teachers sort through problems encountered when students are unable to complete even minimal homework assignments. One problem commonly found in large urban areas is that pupils go home to overcrowded housing conditions, to single parent homes, or to homes in which conflict is rampant. In some cases, students must go home and assume the care of infants or toddlers, and make excuses to protect inebriated or otherwise chemically incapacitated parents from the social service agencies. Obviously, teachers working with these pupils are at a critical disadvantage if the product achievement of their students is used as the measure of teaching effectiveness.

One major step a teacher can take in protecting his rights is to anticipate all factors bearing upon his instruction and to list these. He should then establish the manner in which these factors bear specifically upon the potential outcome of his instruction, and upon the extent to which students are able to master certain product goals. A third step in this process would be to put all of the above in the form of a formal letter to appropriate administrators, with a copy for one's own file, specifying that, in the event of an evaluation focused primarily on product outcomes, the teacher desires that the factors identified in the letter be considered. While school administrators are not bound by law or district policy to consider such factors, the teacher has taken a major step toward protecting his or her rights should there ever be a need to pursue litigation as a result of an unfair, negative evaluation.

Product evaluation may be a valid means of determining whether children are learning what the state wants them to know. But used by itself, it is not necessarily valid proof that an individual is not a good teacher.

Process Criteria. Process criteria in teacher evaluation are specific activities or actions teachers take in the process of instruction. For example, it is generally acknowledged that a good lesson begins with some type of motivational introductory device, activity, or statement. It is also acknowledged by educators that a good lesson should have a review component if it is built upon a preceding lesson. Other activities which constitute good teaching according to process criteria are factors such as using audio-visual aids, involving students in discussion, giving very clear directions, using a review at the end of a lesson, and making sure specific materials are available to students. One state board developed a clearly articulated set of process criteria for evaluating student teachers. A sample of some of these criteria is provided at the end of this section.

These criteria were developed by a committee of representatives from all segments of the educational establishment including administrators, teachers, and teacher educators. It is unusual not to find sets of process criteria where teachers are evaluated formally.

What are the disadvantages of process criteria? For one thing, the teacher might use very unorthodox methods which do not adhere to any of the process criteria favored by a given school district or by a given set of administrators, and nevertheless achieve astounding product results. Or, a teacher may use traditional, back-to-basics methods while his superiors and evaluators prefer newer (although not necessarily better) teaching methods. One of the authors has seen teacher evaluations which read, "this teacher uses methods that went out-of-date 50 years ago," but testing showed that he was getting superior results.

For example, Jesus Christ, who is considered by Christians and by many non-Christians as the greatest teacher who ever lived, never, according to any written record that exists, had a set of behavioral objectives for his "students." Christ used many skillful teaching techniques and many of these parallel teaching techniques in use today—techniques which educators have only recently "discovered." It could be argued, though, that on the basis of process criteria, Jesus Christ was a failure. Consider the following. Some of Christ's lectures were obviously vague, so much so that even His best students had to come to Him after

149

the lecture period to ask Him to explain the lesson. In their frustration, they asked why He used teaching methods which caused confusion. He admitted that He had done so deliber- ately—that His teaching methods were chosen specifically so that some of His listeners would not understand! Despite these admissions, no one could argue that Jesus Christ was not an effective teacher. Clearly, process criteria would have been totally inadequate for evaluating the effectiveness of the One whose teaching turned the course of history, changed the destinies of nations, and whose influence continues to constitute the major impact upon contemporary society around the globe. The limitations of process criteria, then, seem clear. It is conceivable that a very good teacher could use very unorthodox processes and still achieve outstanding results. It is this argument, in fact, which is being asserted by the teacher whose case introduces this chapter.

On the other hand, the advantages of process criteria are also clear. First, teachers can be given a set of process criteria ahead of time, preceding the teacher evaluation period. They can attempt to implement the valued processes and, in so doing, demonstrate that they are proficient. It is also possible for professional educators to agree upon what constitutes acceptable teaching processes or procedures. Therefore, there is little room for debate following an unfavorable evaluation about whether such processes or procedures were fair.

Let's suppose that a teacher anticipates that he will be uncomfortable with a number of the processes identified by the district as desirable. The teacher should then specify (again, in writing) to appropriate administrators which process criteria would make the teacher uncomfortable or which would be difficult to implement, and the reasons why. For example, a visually impaired teacher would probably not be able to effectively use an overhead projector if bright light would exacerbate his visual impairment. He could then specify that the use of certain audio-visual aids would be inappropriate for use in his classroom. Another teacher might have developed highly refined skills in the Socratic question and answer technique and not be comfortable with the straight linear exposition of content which includes a motivational introduction, a review, a presentation of material, an eliciting from the students their understanding of material, and a standardized or commonly used application-oriented assignment. In any of the above cases, the teacher should specify what specific processes he or she uses and why these processes seem to be particularly appropriate for his or her class. In most cases, school administrators will be receptive to such suggestions or, even if they are not receptive, they will specify their reasons why they will not accept those teaching procedures as valid. In either case the teacher is forewarned and, heeding the ancient admonition that "forewarned is forearmed," the teacher can take steps to ensure that his rights will be protected and that his interests will be guarded during the evaluation process. Once again, the important thing is that the teacher should very clearly delineate his expectations or his objections to the evaluation process prior to the evaluation. This statement should be in writing, a copy should be kept by the teacher, and copies sent to the appropriate superordinates or other interested parties.

Returning to the example of the teacher who was observed over 40 times in less than one school year period, the whole question of teaching process was the cause of the problem. In this case, a number of other charges against the teacher were listed, but it is import..nt to note that agreement on teaching process would not have been difficult to achieve. Ultimately, the school district does have some right to insist upon certain teaching procedures, and the teacher does have the right to either adopt those procedures and keep his job, or refuse to adopt those procedures and anticipate, justifiably, his termination. However, this right of the school district must be balanced against the teacher's right of academic freedom, at least if the teacher has tenure.

STUDENT TEACHER APPRAISAL REPORT

Student Teacher _____ Subj./Grade _____ Date _____

Principal _____ School _____ District _____

Supervising Teacher _____ College Supervisor _____

Activity Observed _____ Observed from ____ to ____

	OBSERVED	NOT OBSERVED	REPORTED	EVIDENCES

PLANNING AND ORGANIZATION

1. Uses written lesson plans in coordination with supervising teacher.
2. Uses appropriate sequences for learning concepts and skills.
3. Plans for individual needs, learning styles and abilities through activities such as differentiated assignments, tutorial, small and large group instruction.
4. Adjusts physical environment to accommodate learning activities and organizes necessary materials.
5. Provides for health and safety of students.
6. Other (specify):

152

EVIDENCES

	OBSERVED	NOT OBSERVED	REPORTED

INSTRUCTIONAL TECHNIQUES

1. Provides activities which encourage thinking, problem-solving and decision-making.

2. Encourages students to express divergent points of view, originality and creativity.

3. Uses variety of materials, equipment and technology effectively.

4. Communicates instructional objectives to students prior to providing instruction, modeling and practice.

5. Uses variety of presentation techniques such as lecture, discussion, role playing, modeling and higher-lower order questions.

6. Gives clear directions and assignments.

7. Summarizes and clarifies concepts.

8. Provides guided and independent practice directly related to objectives.

9. Uses feedback from students to monitor progress and improve the teaching-learning situation through activities such as questioning, observing, modeling and assessing.

10. Other (specify):

153

EVIDENCES

	OBSERVED	NOT OBSERVED	REPORTED

MANAGEMENT AND MOTIVATION

1. Uses appropriate management techniques to promote self-discipline, responsibility and respect for the rights and property of others.

2. Creates a positive atmosphere for learning and achievement.

3. Sets expectations, commensurate with student abilities.

4. Generates enthusiasm, stimulates interest and establishes relevance of learning.

5. Uses non-verbal communication effectively.

6. Maximizes student time on task and provides effective pacing and transitions between activities.

7. Makes self available to assist students.

8. Works with students in a fair, consistent manner respecting ideas and differences irrespective of sex, economic status, ethnicity and/or creed.

9. Other (specify):

SUPPORT RELATIONSHIPS

1. Assists in parent conferences when appropriate.

2. Communicates openly and cooperates with supervising teacher and staff.

3. Assists in promoting positive parent and school-community relations.

4. Other (specify):

154

PERSONAL AND PROFESSIONAL DEVELOPMENT

	OBSERVED	NOT OBSERVED	REPORTED	EVIDENCES
1. Demonstrates proficiency in content areas, basic skills and oral and written communications.				
2. Demonstrates professional commitment such as maintenance of confidentiality, awareness of legal requirements and attendance at faculty and inservice meetings.				
3. Demonstrates intellectual curiosity, initiative, loyalty, punctuality, flexibility and positive self-concept.				
4. Adheres to school requirements for dress and grooming.				
5. Other (specify):				

<u>SUMMARY STATEMENTS/RECOMMENDATIONS:</u>

Conference Date _____   Signature: Student Teacher _____

Signature: College Superviser _____   Signature: Supervising Teacher (optional) _____

MP-6-85 Colorado Department of Education S.T.A.R. project funded through Council of Chief State School Officers by the Mellon Foundation.

Teacher Evaluation: Your Legal Rights

Fortunately, educators from all levels of education have become increasingly aware of the necessity to conduct not only fair evaluations, but ones which will also have a positive effect upon the teaching/learning environment and upon the careers of teachers who are dedicated professionals. In a number of states, this awareness has translated itself into state-adopted statutes bearing upon teacher evaluation. Where such statutes exist, the evaluation process is very clearly defined, complete with references to teachers' rights, teachers' responsibilities, and the powers and limitations prescribed and proscribed for evaluators themselves. Although school districts will, no doubt, add their particular nuances of interpretation to the law, in general, state statutes pertaining to teacher evaluation are unambiguous and thorough. For purposes of this discussion, a brief synopsis of a Colorado statute relative to teacher evaluation is offered as an example of what teachers ought to look for or ought to strive for concerning teacher evaluation and the protection of their rights.

The rights of teachers in Colorado are protected when it comes to evaluation by a state statute called "The Certificated Personnel Performance Evaluation Act." Passed in 1984 by the Colorado Legislature, the law was supported by parents and professional groups concerned about teacher effectiveness. The act mandates that every Colorado school district have a sound, credible system for the performance evaluation of certificated personnel, including all teachers and all administrators. The law required all systems to be operational July 1, 1986.

The Performance Evaluation Act requires that all certificated personnel, including non-tenured teachers, be evaluated. The purposes of evaluation, stated in the law, are the improvement of instruction, implementation of the curriculum, measurement of the professional growth of employees, and evaluation of their performance. By law, each district's evaluation system must include:

- The frequency and duration of evaluations, ensuring that sufficient data will be collected from which to draw reliable conclusions and findings;
- No electronic devices without prior consent;
- The evaluation criteria for all teachers including non-tenured teachers;
- The methods of evaluation, including at least direct observations by the evaluator and a process of systematic data gathering;
- Observance of the legal and constitutional rights of all certificated personnel.

The law also requires that a report be issued upon completion of an evaluation. The evaluation report must:
- Be written;
- Contain a written improvement plan stating specifically the employee's strengths and weaknesses and the recommendations necessary for improvement;
- Identify the evaluator's data sources and times of direct observations;
- Be discussed and signed by the evaluator and the employee and then be reviewed by the administrator's supervisor.

The law also provides that evaluators be evaluated on their ability to make fair, professional, and credible evaluations of their employees. The Performance Evaluation Act identifies two groups that play active roles in the implementation of the law. The State Certificated Personnel Performance Evaluation Council developed guidelines to assist school districts in the development of their evaluation systems.

Every school district is also required to have an advisory local council, comprised of teachers, administrators, non-parent residents, and parents. The local council's job is to consult with the school board on the fairness, effectiveness, and quality of the district's evaluation system.

The state council provided the following guidelines to districts to use in the development of evaluation systems:

- Administrators should be trained to acquire critical evaluation skills;
- Evaluation criteria should be related to the employee's job description and the expected outcomes for the position;
- The employee must be informed in advance about the system and criteria for evaluation;
- Hearsay information is not considered acceptable evaluation data;
- The frequency, duration, and cycle of evaluations should be specified, the cycle guaranteeing at least one evaluation every year for non-tenured teachers. Additional evaluations not previously specified should be conducted only for good and just cause. [1]

What To Do If You Receive a Negative Evaluation

A negative evaluation is cause for filing a protest, unless the teacher is absolutely convinced that the evaluation is accurate and one should leave teaching. That, of course, would be a highly unusual situation. The first thing a teacher receiving an unfavorable evaluation ought to do is to follow the procedures outlined in specific statutes pertaining to evaluation. In the absence of such statutes, he can follow the procedures outlined in district policies relative to protesting an unfavorable evaluation. Obviously, statutes and policies will vary from state to state and from locality to locality. Nevertheless, in order for a protest to be given careful consideration, it *must* adhere to policies and procedures relating to protests. It would be unfortunate to have a valid protest dismissed on the grounds that it was improperly filed or did not follow carefully delineated procedures for the filing of a protest. As with any grievance, most districts have a well-defined policy for filing a grievance. This policy should *always* be adhered to, regardless of whether the grievance involves evaluation or some other facet of the teaching responsibility.

If a teacher receives an unfavorable evaluation and decides to file a grievance, certain other general rules ought to be followed in order to make the assertion of the teacher's rights as strong as possible and in order to pave the way for a successful court challenge should such a challenge be necessary. The following guidelines were produced by a local chapter of the National Education Association. Regardless of whether one agrees with various philosophical positions or goals of the NEA, it can be readily established that the National Education Association has been very effective in protecting teachers' rights across the country. Christian teachers can benefit by following many of the guidelines developed by the National Education Association for protecting the rights of teachers as long as these guidelines do not violate a teacher's conscience. One set of guidelines that incorporates many of the preceding suggestions offered in this chapter and adds additional nuances to the filing of a rebuttal to a negative evaluation has been presented by a local Educational Association affiliated with the NEA. This set of guidelines, if followed, can greatly strengthen a teacher's position in challenging a negative evaluation.

When It's Necessary To Write An Evaluation Rebuttal

The teaching staff member's reaction to the annual performance report may take the form of a rebuttal statement. A rebuttal may also be written as a response to *any written or verbal* review of a teacher's performance.

Rebuttals are written so that the teacher's impressions, reactions and additional information are on the record. The rebuttal refutes and counters inaccuracies, misconceptions, erroneous statements, and any item in the evaluation deemed as misleading or disparate. The information included in a rebuttal statement may be helpful in some future proceeding instituted against a teacher or it may simply correct the record or provide additional information for the evaluator's further review.

CEA urges teachers to follow the general guidelines listed below for effective rebuttal writing.

1. Seek advice from your local association and/or UniServ in drafting a rebuttal statement.

2. Before writing any rebuttal, review the contract provisions and/or board policies governing teacher evaluation, reprimand procedures, just cause, etc. In some cases, it may not be advantageous to write a rebuttal. Other avenues may be followed.

3. Utilize the facts as they occurred to develop a statement which is in your best interest. Rebuttals should not be sarcastic or accusative.

4. Require specifics rather than generalities from administrators in evaluation reports.

5. Negative comments may relate to: (a) an improper administrative act; (b) failure of the district to provide the proper assistance and/or materials; (c) circumstances beyond the control of the classroom teacher.

6. Always indicate when administrative assistance was requested but not provided.

7. Request the administration to demonstrate the type of teaching techniques it wants you to incorporate into your lessons.

8. The rebuttal should emphasize any contractual and/or legal violations in the procedures allowed by the administration.

If you have any questions, contact your UniServ Director.

WRITING THE REBUTTAL

Consider the following steps in writing a rebuttal:

1. *Analyze* the observation/evaluation.

    a. Give an overview of the document as to its being negative, positive, slanted, self-serving for the evaluator, etc.

    b. Document areas of negativism in observation/evaluation.

    c. Attempt to discern a pattern, form or context of items checked on the evaluation form and written in the narrative.

    d. Select those items which need correction by rebuttal.

    e. Mention any failures on the part of the evaluator to appropriately and specifically relate performance criteria.

2. *Neutralize* all items which need rebuttal.

a. Give reasons for performance in the items evaluated negatively.

b. Give rationale for activity performance, lesson plan, lesson content and other items which have been criticized. Refer to class size, constraints, available materials and/or district resources.

c. Answer in rebuttal any item mentioning the words or phrases "failure to do," "lack of," "in need of," "should/could have," "suggest," "noticed," or "appeared."

d. Mention any failures on the part of the evaluator to appropriately and specifically relate performance criteria.

3. *Equalize* the results.

The rebuttal should be structured so as to strengthen performance and weaken the negative items on the observation/ evaluation report. Some of the following might be considered:

a. Stress preparation, motivation, curriculum and lesson flow.

b. Focus on objectives, procedures, and attainment.

c. Be clear in directions, assignments, and closing of lessons.

d. Connect all performance with curriculum and job description.

e. If the evaluator failed to help or demonstrate, mention this.

f. Be critical of, but don't reject, recommendations.

g. Review prior observations and evaluations and use the content of those reports to your advantage.

4. *Utilize* the statements below which best categorize the areas needing rebuttal to introduce your response to each negative item.

a. The objectives, goals, standards or rules cited are so broad as to be void because of vagueness.

b. The wrongs cited exceed the jurisdiction of the school board (e.g. beard, home life, etc.), which is limited to the orderly, safe, and efficient operation of the school district.

c. The cited prohibitions violate consitutional guarantees

to my free speech, association, political advocacy, or to the standards of academic freedom accepted in the profession.

d. The cited facts in the evaluation are inaccurate.

e. The evaluation fails to consider constraints of pupil background, overcrowding, school conditions, etc.

f. The evaluator is not competent to evaluate in my field and/or lacks understanding of current acceptable pedagogical practice or board policy or law.

g. My evaluator relied on hearsay.

h. My evaluator failed to observe me for a sufficient amount of time to make a valid judgment.

i. My evaluator failed to give me adequate forewarning of this downrating in that he did not give me sufficient time or assistance to improve, specify the incompetent performance or unprofessional conduct with such particularity as to furnish me an opportunity to correct, or offer specific suggestions and recommendations for improvement.

j. This evaluation is excessive for the wrongs cited.

k. This evaluation fails to consider extenuating and mitigating circumstances.

l. This evaluation is irrelevant to my fitness to teach in that the wrongs cited do not adversely affect students or coworkers to any material degree.

m. This evaluation is inequitable or discriminatory in that the cited standards or rules have not been consistently enforced at my school.

n. I am being downrated for an assignment outside my field.

o. I was given no opportunity to confront accusers.

p. Insufficient consideration was given to my motives.

q. An evaluation may be improper if done by a member of the teacher's bargaining unit.

r. The standards or rules cited are unreasonable, arbitrary, capricious, and/or impossible of observance or attainment. [2]

The preceding guidelines incorporate many of the suggestions that have been offered throughout the chapter, and they address certain specific provisions outlined in the *Colorado* state statute. It is necessary for a teacher to adapt those portions of the guidelines to specific state statutes or local district policies under which he works. In any communication between the teacher and individuals or agencies which might affect the teacher's ultimate rights, copies of all correspondence should be kept. They should be very carefully dated, and in some cases, a return receipt should be requested to validate that the communication was received by the individual to whom it was addressed, as well as the date upon which it was received. Copies should be sent to all individuals or agencies who could conceivably be included in any formal grievance proceeding or formal litigation.

Summary

Few people, professionals or otherwise, would deny that the whole subject of teacher evaluation is one which evokes controversy and which is fraught with emotional stress for those being evaluated, as well as for those doing the evaluation. Some professional organizations reject any form of product criteria as totally inappropriate because the student outcomes are affected by too many variables not within the control of the teacher. If process criteria are used, it is important that the teacher insist upon the following conditions: 1) Obviously, the teacher should know ahead of time what the process criteria are; 2) The process criteria should be possible to attain; 3) The teacher should know in advance who will do the evaluation and the form it will take; 4) If out-of-classroom performance is to be evaluated, the teacher should know ahead of time which specific activities are to be considered and the criteria upon which such evaluation is to take place; 5) The teacher should specify, in writing, any objections he has that should be considered by the administration when carrying out such evaluation; 6) The process criteria should be flexible enough to allow for different styles and philosophies of teaching.

It was also pointed out in this chapter that certain states have very carefully articulated statutes pertaining to teacher evaluation, and that it is very important for a teacher to be thoroughly conversant with these and with local district policy pertaining to evaluation.

Finally, in challenging an unfair or unfavorable evaluation, all communication pertaining to evaluation should be done *in writing*, with duplicate copies, in anticipation of the potential for a formal grievance procedure or litigation in the courts.

Anytime evaluations are conducted, it is a temptation to impose unwarranted comparisons upon teachers. One teacher is cited as being outstanding while another is regarded as mediocre, or certain teachers are selected to receive tangible rewards for their teaching excellence. Such comparisons may be especially repugnant to Christian teachers who accept that their gifts of teaching and their professionally acquired skills are God-given. They recognize that comparisons with others whose skills and abilities are equally God-given are totally erroneous and nonedifying. The authors firmly subscribe to the admonition of the Apostle Paul in Galatians 6:4. The Christian teacher's level of satisfaction with what he may or may not be able to do should be directly related to the extent to which he is doing the best he can with the gifts God has given him.

FOOTNOTES

[1] *The Advisor.* Vol. 6, #5, Jan. 1987 (North Central Colorado Teachers Association) pp. 6 & 7. Reprinted by permission.
[2] *The Advisor.* Vol. 6, #3, Nov. 1986 (North Central Colorado Teachers Association) p. 7. Reprinted by permission.

Sources of Help

Sources of Help

The Battle for Religious Liberty, Lynn R. Buzzard, Samuel E. Ericsson, Elgin, Illinois: David C. Cook Publishing Co., 1982.

Best Reference Books, Bordan Wynar, ed., Littleton, Colorado: Libraries Unlimited, 1986.

Better Late Than Early, Raymond and Dorothy Moore, New York: *Reader's Digest*—Hewitt, 1976.

Bible-Science Newsletter, Bible-Science Association, 2911 East 42nd St., Minneapolis, Minnesota 55406. (The Bible-Science Association can supply current lists of good materials on creationism or the question of origins.)

The Christian Legal Advisor, John Eidsmoe, Grand Rapids: Baker Book House, 1984, 1987.

The Christian Teacher and the Public Schools, Christopher Hall, Oak Park, Illinois: Christian Legal Society, 1975, 1978 supplement by John W. Whitehead.

Christianity and the Constitution: Faith of Our Founding Fathers, John Eidsmoe, Grand Rapids: Baker Book House, 1987.

Classrooms in Crisis: Parents' Rights and the Public Schools, Arnold Burron, John Eidsmoe, Dean Turner, Denver: Accent, 1986.

The Constitution and American Education, Arval A. Morris, St. Paul: West Publishing Company, 1980.

Discipline That Can't Fail, Arnold Burron, Grand Rapids: Baker Book House, 1984.

Encyclopedia of Educational Research, Harold E. Mitzel, ed., Toronto, Ontario: The Macmillan Company, Collier-Macmillan Canada, Ltd., American Research Associates, Fifth Edition, 1982.

"Equal Access IS the Law," Christian Legal Society.

The Freedom of Religious Expression in the Public High Schools, John W. Whitehead, Westchester, Illinois: Crossway, 1983, 1984.

Handbook of Reading Research, P. David Pearson, New York: Longman, Inc., 1984.

Home Built Discipline, Raymond and Dorothy Moore, Waco, Texas: Word Books, 1987.

Home Grown Kids, Raymond and Dorothy Moore, Waco, Texas: Word Books, 1981.

Home Spun Schools, Raymond and Dorothy Moore, Waco, Texas: Word Books, 1982.

The International Encyclopedia of Education, New York: Pergamon Press, Ltd., 1985.

The Law of Public Education, E. Edmond Reutter, Jr., and Robert R. Hamilton, Mineola, New York: Foundation Press, 1976.

NEA: The Trojan Horse in American Education, Samuel Blumenfeld, Boise, Idaho: Pardigm, 1984.

The Parent Educator and Family Report, Hewitt Research Foundation, P.O. Box 9, Washougal, Washington 98671-0009.

Reading: Tests and Reviews, Oscar Buros, ed., Highland Park, New Jersey: The Gryphon Press, 1975.

The Religious Freedom Reporter, published monthly by the Center for Law and Religious Freedom, P.O. Box 1492, 6901 Braddock Road, Springfield, Virginia 22151.

Review of Research in Education, Edmund Gordon, ed., Washington, D.C.: American Education Research Associates, 1985.

School Can Wait, Raymond and Dorothy Moore, Washougal, Washington: Hewitt, 1979.

School Law, Kern Alexander, St. Paul, Minnesota: West Publishing Company, 1980.

Schools: They Haven't Got a Prayer, Lynn R. Buzzard, Elgin, Illinois: David C. Cook Publishing Co., 1982.

State, School and Family, Michael S. Sorgen, William A. Kaplin, Patrick S. Duffy, Ephraim Margolin, New York: Matthew Bender, 1979.

Textbooks on Trial, James C. Hefley, Wheaton, Illinois: Victory Books, 1976, 1977.

What Are They Teaching Our Children? Mel and Norma Gabler with James C. Hefley, Wheaton, Illinois: Victor Books, 1985.
Winchell's Guide to Reference Books, Eugene Sheehy, ed., Chicago, Illinois: American Library Association, 1980.

Other Sources of Help

If a problem at school has the potential of becoming too difficult for you to handle, it is wise to consult a lawyer. Remember also: A lawyer may be very capable in one field but utterly incompetent in another. Asking a securities lawyer to handle a First Amendment religious freedom case might be like asking a podiatrist to perform brain surgery!

If you retain a lawyer, you should expect to pay him, although you may be entitled to legal services through your employment. Some employees' contracts include pre-paid legal services as a fringe benefit. Check to see if yours does, and if so, whether it includes this type of case. Also, in many cases the teachers' union—the local affiliate of the National Education Association or the American Federation of Teachers—will provide representation in a job-related matter. Often they are obligated to do so whether they want to or not. You may be entitled to this service even if you do not belong to the NEA or AFT.

Several organizations exist for the purpose of helping Christians on cases involving religious freedom. One is the Christian Legal Society, P.O. Box 1492, Merrifield, Virginia 22116-1492, (703) 560-7314. CLS, through its affiliate the Center for Law and Religious Freedom, keeps a file of legal briefs and other helpful materials which they supply to lawyers in religious freedom cases.

The National Legal Foundation, P.O. Box 64845, Virginia Beach, Virginia 23464, (804) 424-4242, organized under the sponsorship of CBN Ministries, helps Christians in religious freedom issues.

Concerned Women for America, founded by Beverly LaHaye,

has a legal staff eager to assist Christians. CWA may be reached at 122 "C" St. N.W., Suite 800, Washington, D.C. 20001, (202) 628-3014.

The Rutherford Institute, P.O. Box 510, Manassas, Virginia 22100, was founded by John W. Whitehead. The Institute vigorously defends Christian schools and home schools and actively fights abortion.

The Creation-Science Legal Defense Fund, P.O. Box 78312, Shreveport, Louisiana 71137 is defending the Louisiana law which provides balanced treatment of origins in public school classrooms. The Fund may be willing to assist others who suffer discrimination because of their creationist beliefs.

The Christian Law Association, 100 Erieview Plaza, 34th Floor, Cleveland, Ohio 44114, (216) 696-3900, defends private schools and home schools and may assist in a public school matter.

The Catholic League for Religious and Civil Rights, 1100 West Wells Street, Milwaukee, Wisconsin 53233, (414) 289-0170, represents Catholics on religious freedom matters and occasionally represents others as well.

Mel and Norma Gabler have founded Educational Research Analysts, P.O. Box 7518, Longview, Texas 75607, (214) 753-5993. They analyze public school textbooks page-by-page and report on the strengths, weaknesses, humanistic and anti-Christian biases found therein.

Eagle Forum, founded by Phyllis Schlafly, actively assists Christians in the public arena by educating them on current moral issues and lobbying for good legislation. Eagle Forum may be reached at Box 618, Alton, Illinois 62002, (618) 462-5415.

The Christian Educators Association International, P.O. Box 50025, Pasadena, California 91105, (213) 684-1881, actively serves and encourages Christian teachers in public and private education through seminars, practical advice, and so on. Their publication, *Vision*, is a "must" for Christian teachers and is sent regularly to members.

The National Council for Better Education, 1373 Van Dorn Street, Alexandria, Virginia 22304, (703) 684-4404 is a conservative Christian counterpart to the NEA.